$3000+ A MONTH PART-TIME ON EBAY

Mike Chambers

Mary K. Chambers

Abidian Books

$3000+ a Month Part-Time on eBay

Published by Abidian Books
1937 W Palmetto Street #181
Florence, SC 29501
info@abidian.com

ISBN-13: 978-1981240494
ISBN-10: 1981240497

Printed in the United States of America

A lot of times, people don't know what they
want until you show it to them.

Table of Contents

Foreword

Got a lot of "stuff" you don't need? Want to clean up and bring in a little extra money in the process? That is exactly how the two of us started with eBay. We quickly became what eBay calls a "Top Rated Seller" consistently bringing in over $3,000 a month. In this book, we share some insight about the things that worked ... and some that didn't. It's our story and now it can be yours as well.

In most any successful journey, there are people that help and support you. Our journey is no different.

Kay's best friend Barbie and her daughter Ana were there for us with ideas and acting as a sounding board. At times we learned together. At times they taught us. It was awesome to have someone close in about the same stage in their online efforts sharing their own trials and tribulations.

We also benefited from resources like YouTube and Facebook. From how to package an item to handling returns, there are a lot of good people sharing sound advice. After a while, we learned there were also a lot of people on YouTube and Facebook sharing bad advice. In retrospect, the two sites were a mixed blessing for us. When you're just starting, most any help is thought to be a good thing. After you've stubbed a toe or two, you learn some advice may not have been so good after all. There's no doubt YouTube and Facebook helped us be successful quicker. For that, we're grateful and appreciative.

Our biggest source of learning came internally from our own hands-on problem solving. It was through our problem-solving efforts we had some of our greatest and most beneficial learnings. This was the case from packaging to customer service.

So, sit back, enjoy and we hope you are even more successful than we were in starting an eBay business!

Kay and Mike

Clearing Out the Junk

Housecleaning

We've been married for several years and have always lived in the same home. As we've never moved, we had collected quite a bit of "stuff." For the two of us, our eBay adventure really began with the desire to do a bit of housecleaning. At one time, Kay owned a brick-and-mortar bookstore. She sold most of the books from the store but over time her collection had grown once again. Kay sorted through her books and stored those she didn't have a need for in boxes. The books were a good example of our "stuff." Our bookcases were full and we had boxes of books all over our home. Given their inaccessibility, we couldn't read those books even if we wanted to.

We should also add our children are grown and out on their own. Instead of growing, we're much more in the mode of downsizing. So, what to do with all these boxes of books? Initially, we gave books to the local non-profits. We also tried a garage sale or two. Despite knowing the non-profits were benefiting, it was painful to give away our books. This was especially true for our professional books that we had originally paid a small fortune.

After the bookstore, Kay sold books on Amazon. That seemed to work but for the effort involved, Amazon seemed to be the only one profiting. Amazon also pretty much limited us to books. We had other items we'd like to sell. Kay had also long ago sold an item or two on eBay. eBay scared us though. Both of us had been burned on eBay.

Stepping back, selling our "junk" on eBay carried little risk. If we had an issue with a buyer, the most we would lose would be the cost of shipping. Likewise, we thought if we listed everything at once, only a few weeks of our time would be impacted. We would get rid of our unwanted stuff, make a little money and get on with our life.

Surprise!

Imagine our surprise when the majority of our items started to quickly move … and at an unimagined profit. Given we're retirement-age, we began to wonder if eBay might be a part-time possibility to supplement our income? As they say, the rest is history.

Finding Other Items to Sell

Whoa … Let's Get Legal

Understand we're not accountants or lawyers or anything like that. The advice we offer might work for you and it might not. The best thing to do is to always consult a local professional. Depending on where you live, "cleaning out the garage" usually doesn't require a business license. On the other hand, if you are going to sell routinely, you should get a business license and a state resale certificate. Both will keep you legal and are usually relatively inexpensive.

Having a business license also means you'll probably need to pay sales tax. Most of the time your home state will provide an online system that will allow you to do everything electronically. It also means you'll probably need to declare your business income on your annual state and federal income taxes. So, before going any further, now is a good time to consult a qualified tax professional. Again, we're not experts. Please find someone who is.

Keep in mind a resale certificate will also prove handy in trying to enter the wholesale market when trying to become a "reseller." Manufacturers and true wholesalers usually don't sell to the public. Unlike a retail store, they also don't usually charge sales tax when they sell to a reseller. Again, consult a qualified tax professional.

What's a Good Item to Sell?

To begin our discussion on how to "source" or locate items to sell, it would be wise to first talk about the kind of items that make sense (i.e., are profitable) to sell on eBay.

Size and weight are considerations because the items will usually need to be mailed. If the size is large, it will be difficult (read expensive) to ship. Similarly, if an item weighs a lot, it will be expensive to ship. For beginning sellers a good item to sell usually means something that 1) is sturdy enough to "easily" ship and 2) weighs less than one pound or 3) has a maximum dimension in any one direction less than 12 inches and a total volume (length x height x width) less than 66 cubic inches. Okay, that's a bit much! For now, consider small and light items to be preferable. ☺

Books, music CDs and DVDs are good examples of items sturdy enough to ship. They can also be shipped in inexpensive packaging. In addition to being light; books, CDs and DVDs can all be shipped at a relatively inexpensive USPS class known as "media mail." Details about using USPS Media Mail can be found in Addendum 1. Questions can also be asked at the usps.com website or at (800) ASK-USPS (800-275-8777).

Fragile items are expensive to ship, and not properly packaged, run the risk of breakage during shipping. Keep in mind eBay holds the seller accountable for breakage during delivery. For example, shipping dishes, especially fine china place settings, would require considerable packing material and heavier than normal boxes.

One pound is a breakpoint when it comes to shipping by weight. In the United States, less expensive first-class postage requires the item to weigh less than 16 ounces (1 pound). Above 1 pound requires more expensive USPS shipping alternatives like priority shipping. Shippers like FedEx, UPS and DHL also provide options they call SmartPost in which they will ship the item across country and then turn it over to the local postal service for delivery. Given the additional handling requirements, SmartPost tends to be a slower. The cost of SmartPost shipping is often very close to much faster USPS Priority Shipping, especially when taking advantage of the USPS discounted rates provided to eBay.

The odder (and larger) the dimensions of a product, the more difficult it is to ship. This is true even if the item is relatively light in weight. Consider a kite, golf club or a large stuffed animal.

Selling Price Range

If you're bored and looking for something to do, sell inexpensive, less than $5 items. Seriously. The stereotypical eBay buyer is looking for a bargain. Something less than $5 with free shipping is usually thought of as a bargain. Again, if you're bored, this is a great approach. It will keep you busy, especially if you're selling a bunch of items. If you're looking to make a bit of money while not totally consuming your life … well, not so much.

For something to be worth your time to find, list, package and ship it likely needs to be valued at least $15. We would be happier at $50. We would be ecstatic at $100+. Put differently, it's awfully tough to see at least $10 profit on a $5 item. That math doesn't work.

The two of us had conversations along the lines of "we'll sell low-priced things and make it up with volume." Our normal day is to sell a dozen plus items. One day the only thing we sold was two items, both selling for less than $5. The entire trip to the post office we were thinking "Man, this is crazy." That's when we realized selling multiple, inexpensive items was not a good fit for us. Since then we have concentrated on items where we could profit at least $10 per sale.

Wholesale Distributors

With a resale certificate in hand, you can apply to other companies and their wholesale distributors to resell products. You will then have a chance to source inventory to sell on eBay at prices below that offered to the general public.

How much lower will depend on the other party and the amount of business you do with them. Depending on the item and how far up the food chain you go (i.e., a manufacturing company will provide a deeper discount than a distributor). Discounts are all over the map … anywhere from 5% to 90+%.

Ingram Content Group is the largest book wholesaler. Wholesale electronics can be purchased at places like Megagoods and Evertek. Both of the latter seem receptive to working with small resellers. You may also be able to arrange for tax free purchases from some of the larger retail chains. For example, with your resale certificate and as long as you are reselling the item, Sam's Club will sell to you tax free. No, they do not provide a discount to resellers!

> **Power Seller Tip** — **Warehouse Clubs**
>
> Having a reseller's account at a place like Sam's Club will probably not help for normal items. However, "local" items like a nearby university's souvenirs and apparel or items in a Sam's Club clearance area could be another story.

Going Out of Business Sales

Our local K-Mart went out of business. For several weeks prior to actually closing the store, they kept reducing the prices of the remaining items. Especially near the end, we were able to pick up some nice bargains. An example would be steel-toe work boots. We paid $5 and later sold them for $30.

We also bought some mouth guards at K-Mart. It doesn't matter how good the price is if they don't sell. Months later, we had sold one mouth guard. Regardless of the deal we might think we're getting, those mouth guards taught us to do a bit of market research before making even the smallest of investment in items to sell. That could be as simple as scanning the item bar code and seeing if it is selling on eBay. See the *Managing Your Finances* chapter for additional details.

Another consideration with a going out of business sale is the amount of discount provided. In addition to K-Mart, our local Toys 'R Us went out of business. Initially, both K-Mart and Toys 'R Us marked up their prices. During our first visits, the prices were well above listed prices elsewhere. It wasn't until near the actual closing date that bargains were available.

Overstock Chains

There is a difference between "overstock" stores and stores that handle salvage and returns. In general, avoid open-box returned items. At best, if it works, returns can be sold as used. If the return doesn't work, you're likely out the cost of the purchase as those types of stores usually have a limited return policy.

> **Power Seller Tip** — **Seller Refurbished**
>
> Some resellers that go the returns/salvage route, list the condition of their items as "Seller Refurbished". To an experienced (read skeptical) buyer, this means the seller acquired or had a return they "fixed." Instead, test the item to the best of your ability, and then list it as used or pre-owned.

Similar to returns is the salvage market. Unless you're quite handy at repairs and the potential profit is high (i.e., hundreds to thousands of dollars per sale), salvaged merchandise is another area for most resellers to avoid.

On the other hand, overstock chains carry surplus inventory that could not be handled or sold at a conventional retail outlet. It varies with the chain, but the products tend to be new and factory-sealed.

The most widely known overstock chain is overstock.com. There is also a brick and mortar chain known as Ollie's Bargain Outlet located in the eastern part of the United States. Overstock items can also be found in the "clearance" area of many retail stores. Walmart's yellow clearance aisles are a good example. A similar clearance area exists in many Sam's Clubs, Office Depots and Home Depots. Again, factory-sealed items are preferred versus an open-box that could be a defective return.

Library Sales

Most public libraries have limited shelf space. To keep their shelves fresh and up-to-date, they frequently have book sales to move old, less-used books.
A library may also have multiple copies of what was once a popular title. Over time, the popularity falls off and so does the need for so many copies.

It varies but expect to pay anywhere from 10 cents to a dollar or two per item at a library book sale.

When it comes to books, the profit is often higher for non-fiction than fiction or children's books. First editions of classics and current textbooks can be among the best resell items in terms of profitability. See the book section of Addendum 2 – BOLOs for additional suggestions.

Thrift Stores

Understand thrift stores tend to be non-profits. Do not expect bright lights, spotless rest rooms and the latest fashions. Also, appreciate others before you have likely scanned their clothing, household items, books, videos and music CDs. Every now and then a jewel can be found in those areas but they tend to be well picked. Some of the larger chains like Goodwill also scan their books. Notice there are quite a few Goodwill sellers on both eBay and Amazon.

A more fruitful opportunity in thrift stores may be items like tools, electronics, housewares, jewelry or shoes. We have found some awesome bargains in tools, electronics and shoes. One bargain that comes to mind is a $25 purchase of Bose speakers. In a very quick flip, we made several hundred dollars on our purchase.

Garage Sales, Estate Sales and Flea Markets

Better than thrift stores might be garage sales, estate sales and flea markets. With garage and estate sales, the seller often doesn't realize the value of what they are selling. To them it may be consuming needed space and they just want to get rid of it. Such a mentality can make for great bargains.

Flea markets can be a little different. Sometimes, you may stumble across "garage sales" who had rather rent a table than have folks drop by their home. More often, you will find other resellers and craft people. We love the crafts, especially woodworking, so we don't mind too much. Just remember they've paid rent for a table and have costs associated with their work. Expect their prices to be less than retail but not thrift store or garage sale levels.

Online Suppliers

All it takes is a website and you too can become an online supplier. ☺

We haven't had much success here. Fundamentally, you will likely need a search engine to find an online supplier. If you can find an item in a search engine, non-reselling customers can as well.

Liquidation Websites

Like salvage companies, be leery of open/returned merchandise. There is a liquidation website we stumbled across that sells tools. They are buying open box returns by the truckload from one of the national tool stores. Again, at best, if it worked, you would be selling at used prices.

BULQ is a liquidation website that has everything from brand new to salvage merchandise. On YouTube, it's probably the most popular of the liquidation sites. In business since 2004, their merchandise categories include brand new, like new, uninspected returns, scratch and dent, and salvage. Goods can be purchased by the case (roughly 20" x 23" x 24") or pallet (roughly 40" x 42" x 48"). Shipping to a residential address is not an issue. Notifications are available via their mobile app (Apple and Android) when new inventory listings match desired category and condition preferences. On the down side, they do not offer returns or exchanges. Quantifying the current market value of a given lot can also be a time consuming, if not fruitless, challenge.

Government liquidation websites (like govliquidation.com and govdeals.com) can be viable but be careful. Items can be dated (e.g., laptops that are 10 years old). Frequently, the government websites also require purchasing in at least pallet-size loads. Pallet-size purchases are something to think about but do not let yourself miss a good bargain. We purchased an inexpensive flatbed trailer we pull behind our SUV. The trailer quickly paid for itself and also came in handy moving a friend and carrying items like building supplies for other activities.

Alibaba (China)

We suppose if you are on the front-end of the next "pet rock," Alibaba could be awesome. You can also have them re-brand items with your logo. It could be a proud moment sharing with friends and family. Surprise: our experience has been beyond Mom and Dad, a USB drive with our logo on it isn't going to sell any better than one without a logo … even with friends, and especially with family members other than Mom and Dad!

As we have tried to source items through Alibaba, we have found the prices to be low on the surface until we add necessities like shipping the items to the states and paying customs taxes. In general, to spread out the shipping costs, significant inventories and pallet-size orders are required.

In the end, there just wasn't enough margin to be profitable, especially when we were going to have to compete against China-based resellers already on eBay. There are also potential language, quality and warranty issues. Usually, if there is an issue, you are responsible for shipping the item back to China. In our feeble minds there is a problem with someone selling you a defective product and you having to spend even more to get it corrected.

A lot of people claim to make money with overseas suppliers. We're certainly not experts. Obviously, your mileage may vary from our experience!

BOLOs

Regardless of where you source, a BOLO list may prove helpful. BOLO is an acronym for Be On the Look Out.

BOLO lists for books, electronics, clothing and toys can be found in Addendum 2.

Pricing

It does no good to locate a great buy and not be able to sell it. We cringe when we hear words like "I don't know what I'm going to do with it but it was such a great buy, I couldn't pass it up!" Earlier in this chapter, we shared our own experience with mouthguards.

Before purchasing an item, it's just good common sense to have a reasonable feel for its value and how you would resell it. New resellers are often hesitant to bring out their phones in the middle of a store or conversation. We feel the same way. That's called being polite and please don't stop doing it. What we do is get off to the side (like you're checking your e-mail!) and check the item on at least eBay. It's not enough to see if there are any listings. You should also see if any have sold. We know … details! ☺

Getting Started at eBay

Why eBay?

Ummm, because this book is about eBay. ☺

Seriously, there are a number of online marketplaces including Amazon, Poshmark, Mecari, Jet, uBid and Walmart. Great selling experiences can be had at all of them but outside of Facebook or Craigslist, eBay tends to be one of the easiest in terms of start-up. eBay also tends to have more potential buyers.

It's not free but eBay also has a competitive fee structure that is relatively easy to understand. For example, at the time of publication, a new seller can list up to 50 items for free paying only a roughly 10% final value fee. The 10% is variable based on the item category. PayPal will also charge $0.30 per transaction and 2.9% of the final value. As we write, eBay is in the process of adding a system called Managed Payments to supplement the PayPal option. Soon, eBay sellers will be able to offer payment with Apple Pay and Android Pay. This is important as most purchases are now made by smartphone.

	eBay	Amazon
Selling Price	$10.00	$10.00
Listing Fee	0	0.99
Final Value Fee	-1.00	-1.50
Credit Card/PayPal	-0.59	0
Paid to Seller	$8.41	$7.51

Suppose a new seller sold 40 books at $10 each. The table above illustrates the difference in profitability between Amazon and eBay. Shipping is assumed to be the same for both.

By comparison, Amazon currently charges $0.99 per transaction plus a similar variable fee of roughly 15%. The Amazon fee for books, DVDs and music CDs is 15%. Other items range from a low of 6% for personal computers to as much as 20% for collectibles. Most anything can be sold at eBay while Amazon must approve some items like certified refurbishments and still other items like automotive parts, business-to-business products, food and clothing. The latter items can only be sold by what Amazon calls "professional sellers." Amazon uses a system affectionately referred to as "gating" to prevent most sellers from selling items beyond books. A seller must apply to remove the gate. It's a hassle but Amazon does provide a mobile app that makes the process a bit faster and less cumbersome.

History of eBay

eBay began in 1995 and was one of the more successful darlings of the dot-com boom of those times. A Paris-born computer scientist named Pierre Omidyar started writing code for what ultimately became the backbone for today's ebay.com website.

Pierre Omidyar was the son of an Iranian surgeon and PhD linguistics professor. His parents left Iran in order to obtain a better education in France. When Pierre was young, they again moved, this time to the Maryland where his father worked at Johns Hopkins University. At an early age, Pierre became interested in computers and ultimately graduated with a degree in computer science from Tufts University in Medford, Massachusetts.

On Labor Day, September 4, 1995, Pierre Omidyar launched a person-to-person marketplace he called AuctionWeb. A "broken" laser pointer was the first item sold on the website. By the middle of 1997, AuctionWeb was hosting over 800,000 auctions a day. Later that year, in September of 1997, AuctionWeb became eBay.

In 2018, eBay reported a gross merchandise volume of $95 billion and annual revenue of $10.7 billion. At the end of 2018, across the globe, eBay has over 179 million active buyers with 600 thousand sellers promoting 200 million listings.

eBay from 10,000 Feet

600,000 sellers are a lot of sellers. In any market, that's a lot of competition. The good news is eBay still has niches that can be highly profitable. Being the only seller for a popular item is a good thing. Being one of 300 sellers for an unpopular item … well, not so much.

Today, eBay reports over 80% of the items listed are new. That can make competitively priced used items a potential niche. From tools to electronics to smartphones, eBay can be a very attractive outlet for pre-owned items.

Unlike most other marketplaces, eBay also offers auctions and what they call "best offer." The auctions often start at pennies and run several days. Buyers bid against each other and the clock. When the auction ends, the item is sold to the highest bidder. Best Offers are something of a passive auction where a buyer can make an offer on a fixed price listing. As a seller, you can accept, counter or reject the offer. Although low-ball offers can be a challenge, we have found best offers to be an effective way to move stale merchandise. See the Growth with eBay chapter for additional details on Best Offers.

The eBay Catalog

The eBay Catalog is a relatively new arrangement. It's essentially a database containing product information. That's important as it makes it easier (and quicker!) for a seller to list an item. Amazon uses a similar catalog structure.

Historically, each eBay seller would enter the specs, pictures and UPC for a given item. Compared to the Amazon version of a catalog, this was a relatively time-consuming task. As a result, some sellers would scrimp on things like the specs and pictures.

Another issue with the old way at eBay is many sellers would not list an ISBN for books or UPC for other items. They understood (correctly) that buyers would typically search by the item name. For example, a buyer would search for "Nike running shoes size 11" and not the UPC for those shoes. The only people that used the UPC to search for an item were other sellers. In this way, savvy resellers could list an item that would stay below the radar of many competing sellers. Naively, the sellers searching with UPC bar codes would think they didn't have much competition and price the item accordingly, typically higher.

Such tactics are no longer possible with the catalog. The catalog is driven by ISBNs and UPCs. If you want to list an item and have pictures and specs populate the listing automatically, the only way to make that consistently happen is through the catalog.

The catalog also makes it easier for search engines like Google. With the catalog, a given item has the same general details for all sellers. This can result in sales from customers that were searching offsite using Google.

eBay Resources

eBay Help and the eBay Community are there 24/7. Both can be an effective way to learn. The eBay Community contains like-minded buyers and sellers. One of the neat features is the Community is monitored by eBay and an eBay employee will frequently enter popular conversations to share eBay's perspective.

YouTube and Facebook are also loaded with videos and user groups discussing nothing but eBay. YouTube can be a great resource starting out and learning "how to." Many of the videos are short, concise and well done. Others are plain wrong and some even illegal. Starting out, we didn't know better.

We frankly would not have had the early success we did without YouTube. At times, the videos also shared a way that did not encourage us to learn a perhaps more efficient way. There were also videos that suggested illegal ideas like using free USPS supplies for packing material. Another bad idea we saw was how to reconfigure (i.e., enlarge) the USPS flat rate packaging. Both of the latter suggestions are very much against postal regulations.

Facebook was an equally excellent early resource for asking questions. Some of the Facebook groups have hundreds of thousands of members. A number of people typically respond to a question. There can be some very helpful and insightful responses. As an example, we learned how to handle returns on Facebook.

We ultimately found several issues with Facebook. One is the time drain to keep up with everything occurring in a group. We want to learn the things we don't know (yes, you can quote us!) but had no desire learning that Billy Bob just made his first sale. The second issue is the privacy and tracking shortcomings inherent with Facebook. Everything we read, click on or follow is sold to others. Sure, Google and other companies do the same but the feeling of being invaded is not quite as pervasive. As an example, just look at a Facebook link to an external website. That link contains tracking details that will follow you across the internet. Another issue with Facebook was the confrontational style of some members. Fortunately, the number of those members is relatively small. Whether they are right or wrong, we don't think someone sharing an idea trying to help someone else should ever be attacked.

Google is Your Friend

We also had great success using Google to find answers. In addition to YouTube and Facebook links, there are links to websites, blogs and other repositories, all full with answers. A bit amusing, we have found searching the eBay help pages easier (and faster) with Google than the eBay search engine ... ooops! That's not a knock on eBay as no one compares to Google and the effectiveness of their search engine. Just ask Microsoft and Yahoo ...

An advantage of Google is the search results are prioritized by 1) paid results (not so helpful) and 2) results others found useful (very helpful). The first place we go when looking for information tends to be Google.

The downside of Google is the tracking. Unlike Facebook, it's not as obvious. If you don't think Google is tracking you, visit myactivity.google.com.

Packing and Shipping

Find an Old Amazon Box?

The economics are pretty straightforward. The less spent on packing and shipping, the more profit. So, why not repurpose some of the old Amazon boxes laying around the house? No, you really don't want to do that!

It was Will Rogers that said "You never get a second chance to make a first impression." The packaging is the first impression a buyer has of you and your product. Back to the repurposed Amazon box … what sort of first impression do you think a used Amazon box with three different types of tape is going to make?

It's also not a good idea to use old boxes that contained cleaning supplies or alcoholic beverages. Refer to Section 227 of USPS Publication 52 *Hazardous, Restricted and Perishable Mail.*

Examples of commonly reused boxes include cleaning supply boxes and liquor/wine/beer boxes. Some cleaning products are hazardous materials; although most alcoholic beverages are not hazardous materials, they are prohibited from mailing. Packages containing alcoholic beverages or with alcoholic beverage markings are prohibited in the mail.

There is also the issue of old labels. In addition to being unsightly, they can also be confusing to the carrier. Again, from Section 227 of USPS Publication 52 *Hazardous, Restricted and Perishable Mail* …

> … Because of safety concerns and in compliance with laws governing the transportation of hazardous, restricted, and prohibited materials, as well as privacy statutes, the Postal Service must assume that all markings and labels on a package identify the actual content.

> Reused packaging, boxes and containers that bear inapplicable labels or markings associated with hazardous, prohibited, or restricted materials are prohibited in the mailstream, unless the labels or markings have been removed or completely obliterated. If the labels or markings can still be read or identified, they are not sufficiently obliterated.

Incorrect   Correct

Existing markings, text and labels should be completely removed or obliterated. [Graphic from USPS Publication 52 Hazardous, Restricted and Perishable Mal]

Back in the Day

In the past, it was a common practice to wrap a box in brown paper. Sometimes, it was taped. Sometimes, it was tied with string. Both shipping paper and brown grocery bags were used. The same as with the repurposed Amazon box, don't use brown paper and string either.

The shipping industry has changed dramatically since the days of brown paper packaging. Today's conveyors and sorting machines would catch, especially on the string, but also on loose edges of the paper wrapping. For this reason, some carriers refuse packages wrapped in brown paper.

Sourcing Your Packing Materials

Locating shipping materials may be easier than you might think. The big box, office supply and warehouse stores all carry shipping supplies. They have everything from packing material (bubble wrap and peanuts) to mailers (envelopes) and yes, even shipping boxes. They're also convenient. Think "easy."

We like to keep packing practical, easy ... and inexpensive

A downside of local retailers is the cost. Often, even the warehouse stores are more expensive than what is available online. The selection is also not going to be nearly as comprehensive. Some of the retailers also put their name on their shipping boxes. We're not sure which would be worse: receiving an eBay purchase in an Amazon box or a Walmart box.

The internet is also a good source of shipping materials. Uline has about the largest selection anywhere. They also produce an excellent catalog that can be a great reference when brainstorming. eBay and Amazon also have a wide selection and their prices tend to be competitive.

Yet Another Source: The USPS Postal Store

When shipping using the United States Postal Service's priority mail class, an eBay seller can use free shipping supplies from the online USPS Postal Store at store.usps.com. This includes both boxes and envelopes. Did we mention they are free? They don't cost anything either! ☺

It would be difficult to find a better price but there is a catch. The free supplies from the Post Office and its online store can only be used to ship items using USPS Priority Mail. There is a notice to that effect on each box and envelope.

 Padded Flat Rate Envelope
EP14PE July 2013
ID: 9.5 x 12.5
  UNITED STATES POSTAL SERVICE.

It reads …

> This packaging is the property of the U. S. Postal Service and is provided solely for use in sending Priority Mail shipments. Misuse may be a violation of federal law. This packaging is not for resale.

Despite what might be seen on YouTube and elsewhere, it is against federal regulations to use items like the padded envelopes as packing material and to reconfigure or modify the supplies in any way. Even if shipping priority mail, a padded priority mailer should not be used to wrap and protect a fragile item and then placed in a second priority mailer.

It is also against the rules to fashion together priority shipping supplies. For example, it would be frowned upon to use several padded priority envelopes taped together to ship a golf club. Items must also fit completely inside and the box or envelope must close on its own without the use of extra tape or a filler. Tape can (and should) be used to make sure the package remains sealed but should never be used to extend the size of the package.

USPS has lost millions on the misuse of shipping supplies. More than ever, they are taking abuse seriously. The United States Postal Service Office of the Inspector General (uspsig.gov) actively investigates postal fraud and abuse. The USPS can also fine customers who misuse priority shipping supplies. An item might also be returned or worse, delivered to a customer with additional postage due. That strikes us as a great way to get yourself in trouble with the law and to ensure negative feedback.

Branded Supplies

Each quarter, eBay store owners are provided a coupon for free eBay-branded shipping supplies. eBay shipping supplies tend to be high-end and we use them on more expensive purchases. They look sharp and do a great job protecting the merchandise.

Having said that, if they weren't free, we probably wouldn't use the eBay supplies. They're more expensive (if we had to buy them) and they are also heavier. Heavier packaging drives up the costs of postage. After one of our eBay-branded shipments disappeared from a buyer's front door, we realized eBay and Amazon packaging also present an inviting target. Given all the disadvantages, we no longer purchase eBay branded supplies beyond what is provided free.

Power Seller Tip — Don't Go Too Cheap!

We don't do it, but a lot of sellers will ship a book, music CD or DVD in a cost-effective 2.0 mil thick white poly mailer.

Instead, we prefer to use a slightly more costly and heavier padded "bubble" envelope. This reduces the potential for damage to the edges of the book, as well as, cracked CD and DVD cases.

Some mailing tapes seem to stick to everything but the package.

Brand-name "heavy duty" shipping tape is also excellent. But like the eBay packaging, it's more expensive and heavier. We use the off-brand tape that is readily available for about $1 a roll. Both stick fine but the less expensive tape is more prone to curl and wrinkle. Again, think first impressions: if you can't get the hang of using the inexpensive tape without it wrinkling, it may be better to use a more expensive tape. Obviously, if the brand of tape chosen does not readily stick, it should be replaced anyway.

Controlling Shipping Costs

There is an art to controlling shipping costs. Easily, our biggest expense beyond the purchase of our inventory is not eBay fees but shipping. As a result, we give considerable thought to how we package and ship our products. See the Kaizen: Hands-On Learning chapter for additional details.

From 10,000 feet, the rates eBay has negotiated with the United States Postal Service (USPS) tend to be better than those eBay negotiated with UPS and FedEx. We don't recall using UPS at all and can count on one hand the times FedEx was less expensive than USPS. When it's available, the USPS media rate is less expensive than USPS First Class. USPS First Class (which only goes to 1 pound) is less expensive than USPS Priority shipments. Our general rule of thumb is to ship USPS media rate if available, then first class if available, and finally, priority.

Power Seller Tip

To help in pricing our items, we created a spreadsheet-based shipping table from the online eBay shipping calculator. We weigh the item, enter it into the spreadsheet and then select the method of shipment. At a glance, we can see what shipping will cost. For convenience, we've also added the eBay and PayPal fees along with the purchase price so we can see, again at a glance, the profit for a given item. A subsection of our profitability spreadsheet can be seen immediately below. A copy of our current shipping table can also be seen below. See the Managing Your Finances chapter for additional details on pricing.

Weight Ex Packaging	Estimated Shipping Cost	List Date	List Price	Margin	Estd Profit
1.5 lb	6.35	Apr-18	32.99	191.01	5.40
1.4 lbs	3.17	Apr-18	15.70	1570.00	9.48
2 lb 2.6 oz	6.35	Feb-18	33.20	167.16	2.99

Shipping cost, along with current eBay and PayPal fees are used to calculate an estimated profit.

Shipping Rates (eBay)
May-19

Lbs.	Oz.	Media	1st Class	1st Class Zone 8
0.0625	1	2.75	2.66	3.09
0.1250	2	2.75	2.66	3.09
0.1875	3	2.75	2.66	3.09
0.2500	4	2.75	2.66	3.09
0.3125	5	2.75	2.79	3.63
0.3750	6	2.75	2.92	3.63
0.4375	7	2.75	3.05	3.63
0.5000	8	2.75	3.18	3.63
0.5625	9	2.75	3.34	4.33
0.6250	10	2.75	3.50	4.33
0.6875	11	2.75	3.66	4.33
0.7500	12	2.75	3.82	4.33
0.8125	13	2.75	4.10	5.53
0.8750	14	2.75	4.38	5.53
0.9375	15	2.75	4.66	5.53
1.0000	16	2.75	4.66	5.53

Lbs.	Media	Priority NYC	Priority LA	FedEx NYC	FedEx LA
Up to 2	3.27	7.40	10.80	10.16	11.24
3	3.79	8.47	15.34	10.50	11.97
4	4.31	8.69	18.15	8.01	10.56
5	4.83	9.37	21.03	11.10	13.07
6	5.35	9.71	24.07	11.98	15.90
7	5.87	10.04	27.04	12.11	16.49
8	6.39	11.33	30.36	12.34	16.91
9	6.91	11.41	33.75	12.45	17.61
10	7.43	13.83	39.76	12.49	18.53
11	7.95	13.82	38.61	12.63	18.57
12	8.47	16.10	42.65	12.71	19.41
15	10.03	18.62	47.57	13.14	22.45
20	12.63	22.43	60.82	14.05	26.60

First Class (Using Stamps)

	Letter*	Lg Flat Rigid
< 1 oz	0.50	3.5
< 2 oz	0.71	3.5
< 3 oz	0.91	3.5
< 3.5 oz	1.12	--
< 4 oz	--	3.5
< 5 oz	--	3.75

Priority

Flat Rate Envelope	6.95
Small Flat Rate Box	7.50
Medium Flat Rate Box	12.80
Large Flat Rate Box	17.60
Padded Flat Rate Env	7.55
Legal Flat Rate Env	7.25

Packing Materials

Label & Packing Slip	0.4 Oz
6 x 10 Padded Env	0.4
10 x 16 Padded Env	1.0
14.25 x 20 Padded Env	1.8
4 x 4 x 4 Box	1.7
7 x 7 x 7 Box	5.0
12 x 10 x 4 Box	8.2
12 x 10 x 8 Box	9.7
1 Sq of Bubble Wrap	0.2

eBay Shipping Supplies

Poly Mailers

6.25 x 8.5	0.2
9 x 11.5	0.4
10 x 12.5	0.5
12 x 15	0.6
14.5 x 18.5	0.8

Padded Mailers

6.5 x 8.75	0.3 Oz
8.5 x 10.75	0.6
9.5 x 13.25	0.9

The above spreadsheet-based table is used to estimate shipping costs. The table was built from the then-current eBay Shipping Calculator.

USPS Zones

The United States Postal Service recently implemented a zone approach to shipping first class and priority. Costs are now based on not only the weight of the package but also how far it is to travel.

Within the lower 48, the worst-case situation would be shipping from one coast to the other. This would be Zone 8, the most expensive in the lower 48. Shipping to a location within 50 miles would be Zone 1 and the least expensive. On a percentage basis, the increases can be dramatic. For example, a 12-ounce first class shipment to Zone 1 would be $3.82 and to Zone 8, $4.33. The zone map for Los Angeles can be seen below.

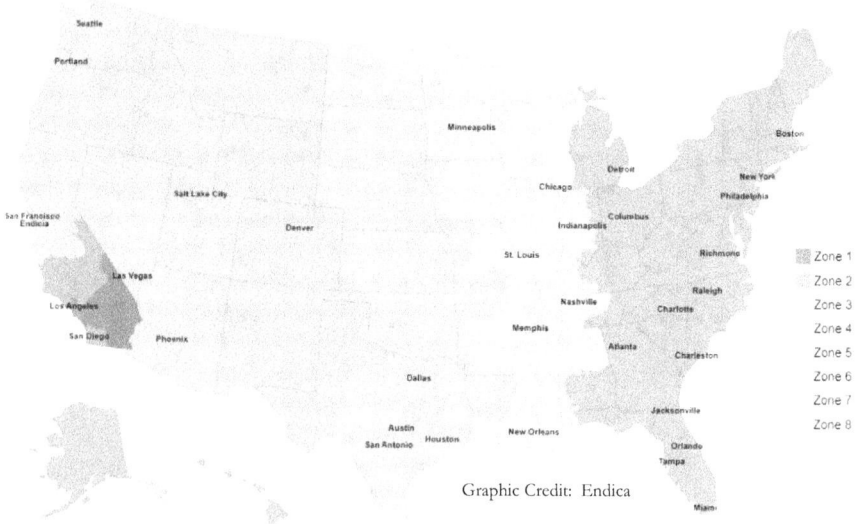

Graphic Credit: Endica

View a dynamic zone map based on your local zip code at apps.endicia.com/apps/zonemap.

Power Seller Tip In light of the USPS shift to zones, base pricing and your shipping estimates on the farthest zone. In the 12-ounce illustration above, we would use the Zone 8 cost of $4.33 to price our item. If it ships closer, that's to our benefit. On the other hand, we would be covered if we had to go across the country. The downside of this approach is sellers in the

Midwest will have a decided cost advantage over those on the East and West coasts. The zone map below is for Topeka, Kansas.

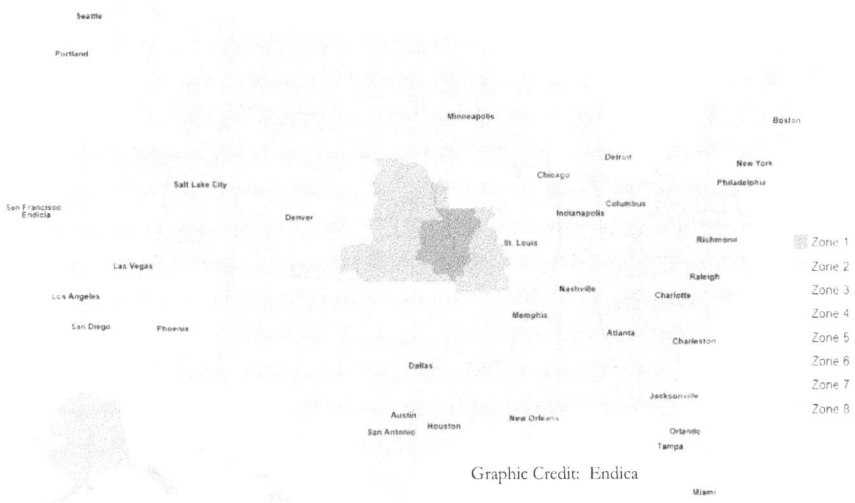

Graphic Credit: Endica

For Topeka, notice most of the country is Zone 6 or less. Alaska and Hawaii are the only areas in Zone 8.

USPS Dimensional Weight

USPS has a relatively new pricing structure taking into account the dimensions of a shipping package. Sellers were previously charged solely on the weight of an item. With Dimensional Weights, the dimensions or volume of the item will also become a factor. From the perspective of USPS, large packages (regardless of their weight) cost more to ship because of the disproportionate amount of space they consume.

USPS Dimensional Weight pricing applies only if three criteria are met:

1) The package weighs more than 1 pound;

2) It is being shipped using Priority, Priority Express or Parcel Select; and

3) The volume of the package exceeds 1,728 cubic inches. For comparison purposes, a 12" x 12" x 12" box has a volume of 1,728 cubic inches.

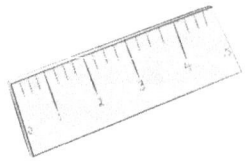 To calculate the Dimensional Weight of a package, multiple the length, width and height to obtain the total cubic inches. Measurements should include any bumps or extrusions and be rounded up. For example, if the length is 11 ½", use 12" in the calculation. Take the product of the length, width and height and, if it's greater than 1,728 cubic inches, divide by 166 to obtain the Dimensional Weight. Again, round up.

If the Dimensional Weight is greater than the actual weight, use the Dimensional Weight to determine the shipping cost. Again, this is only for shipments that are greater than 1,728 cubic inches.

Note UPS and FedEx have been using dimensional weights for domestic shipping. The concept is not new and, if anything, USPS is bringing their service costs in-line with the rest of the shipping industry. UPS also uses a smaller divisor of 139. The smaller divisor will result in a greater dimensional weight (and cost). Although a potential price increase for eBay sellers, the concept of dimensional pricing has already been implemented elsewhere.

A couple of examples will help illustrate the impact. In the first example, suppose we have a 12" x 10" x 8" box weighing 8 pounds.

12" x 10" x 8" = 960 cubic inches

Because the volume is less than 1,728 cubic inches, we use standard weight-based pricing.

In a second example, suppose we have a 14" x 14" x 14" box that weighs the same 8 pounds.

> 14" x 14" x 14" = 2,744 cubic inches

> Because the volume is greater than 1,728, Dimensional Weight pricing applies.

> Continuing, we divide the calculated volume by 166 to obtain the USPS dimensional weight.

> 2744 ÷ 166 = 16.5 pounds … rounded up to 17 pounds.

> Instead of paying the actual weight of 8 pounds, we pay to ship at the 17-pound dimensional rate. This is the weight that should be used in the USPS pricing tables.

Power Seller Tip — Do not underestimate the impact of Dimensional Weight pricing. First, lower your shipping costs by using the smallest possible box that will still protect the item. Even then, expect a dramatic increase on some items. We have a small stuffed animal that was $12 to ship. With Dimensional Weight, the shipping cost is now as much as $60. Although they may be lightweight, large items can be expensive to ship.

Shipping Options

We ship quite a few USPS Priority shipments. For the weights we typically ship, it is more price competitive than FedEx SmartPost. Priority deliveries are also 2-3 days versus 2 to 7 days with a 4-day average for SmartPost.

Power Seller Tip — USPS advertises "if it fits, it ships." Take advantage of their flat rate priority packaging. We have shipped "heavy" orders in $8 flat rate priority packaging that would have cost $30 to $40 to ship in other packaging. A seller can ship up to 70 pounds in each flat rate package.

When it comes to the packaging itself, we prefer the white poly mailers for blister pack items. We like at least a 2.5 mil thickness to minimize holes during transit. For products that might crack (like DVDs), we go with the padded white poly mailers. Some call these air jacket mailers. In addition to being relatively inexpensive, issues with wrinkling tape are also less obvious with the white mailers.

Boxes are our last option as they tend to be heavier and more expensive to buy. Rather than paper packing in a box, we prefer air pillows and peanuts. If a padded mailer or box doesn't fully protect an item, we'll add bubble wrap. The more expensive the item, the greater care we take in packing.

Power Seller Tip Watch the weight by frequently weighing an item as you protect it. As possible, first protect the item but then back off packing to avoid moving into the next rate category. When at the upper limit of a rate, print smaller labels and packing slips to stay at the lowest possible rate.

Power Seller Tip Minimize packing supplies and shipping weights by creative use of the label and packing slip. If you're working with a blister pack product with a cardboard back, place the label and folded packing slip on the blister pack side. This can allow for the use of a thinner, lighter weight poly mailer.

Think Conveyor

As mentioned earlier, shipping companies use conveyors with cameras to move and sort packages. As a result, although not dropped, packages are tumbled and bumped during their journey. The bumps can wear through thin poly mailers. For that reason, we use 2.5 mil or greater mailers. We also try to place the shipping labels in a way that will help protect the edges.

Packages travel along a series of conveyors like that shown above.

**Power
Seller
Tip**

The carrier's cameras must be able to read the package's shipping bar code. If the bar code is smeared or otherwise unreadable, the package must be manually routed adding time to the journey. Carriers frown on the practice but one solution is to put a piece of clear tape over the bar code. When we're forced to tape a bar code, we try to cover only half the bar code leaving the other half open. We also use a matte tape to minimize reflections and glare. The best solution is to use a laser printer, toner and labels that do not readily smear.

**Power
Seller
Tip**

An item sliding and bouncing around within a mailer can also contribute to holing through the mailer and potentially damaging the item. To minimize shifting during transit, we fold the flap further down the mailer to minimize movement. To keep the side openings of the package from catching on the conveyor rails and the like, we use a small amount of tape to keep the openings secure.

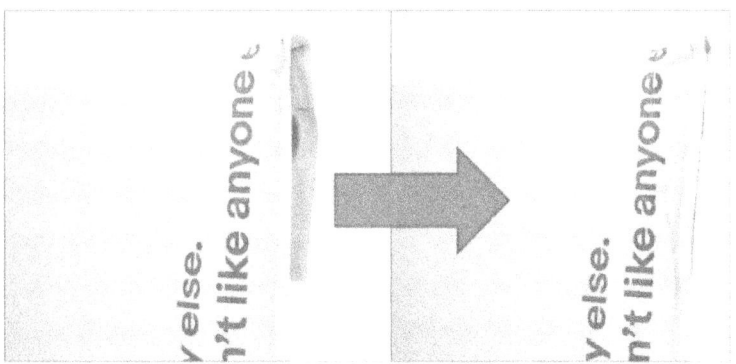

We tape the edges to minimize the chance of the mailer getting snagged on a conveyor. Ideally, we leave a little opening on the top so it can still be easily opened by the buyer.

eBay Subtleties

Buyer Feedback

Our experience is only the selling price is more important than feedback. Consider your own history. When presented with two items that are roughly the same price and condition, which do you choose? If you are like us, we will pay more to deal with a more reliable seller. That's not to say other considerations like the item location and delivery date don't enter the decision but for most, it's price and feedback reputation.

When it comes to buying decisions, price and feedback reputation are the king and queen.

One way to generate positive feedback is to consistently exceed expectations. To quote Larry Page, co-founder of Google, "Always deliver more than expected." If an item is expected in 5 days, deliver it in 3. In lieu of the inexpensive white poly bags, ship in eBay-branded padded mailers. Yet another way to exceed expectations is to have a generous returns policy. Most of the time these selling benefits will cost pennies.

Learn as You Grow

It's important we also learn from and make improvements based on feedback. Bill Gates said it well ... "Your most unhappy customers are your greatest source of learning." Bill is right. Shame on you if corrective steps are not made and the same issue occurs again.

Early on, we received some less than flattering comments regarding some of our listings with multiple items ... eBay calls them variation listings. The gist was the buyer thought they should receive not one but all the items in the listing. When it happened, our initial thought is we were dealing with a sham where the buyer was trying to get something for nothing. As we investigated, we saw how an inexperienced buyer might interpret the listing differently than we intended. It was an easy fix by adding words like "or" in the listing title. This is yet another way we used problem solving in our business. For additional details on our problem-solving process, see the *Hands-On Learning* chapter.

Another example is we were getting some very favorable feedback about our shipping practices when the sale coincided with one of our initial trips to the local post office. Customers like quick shipping. As a result, we shortened our handling time to a day or less and started advertising orders in by noon shipped the same day. 10 AM to noon is now one of our busiest selling times.

The point is learn from customer feedback. Improve the things that aren't the best they can be and continue to grow the things your customers like.

Negative Feedback

Usually, an eBay seller is stuck with negative feedback. However, there are a few situations where a seller can petition eBay and they will remove the feedback. The following are examples of when negative feedback might be removed:

- An item arrives late that you shipped on time (this varies with the customer service rep and your participation in eBay's Guaranteed Delivery Program),
- Tracking indicates an item was delivered yet the buyer claims they did not receive it,
- A buyer changes their order or requests something extra, or
- A buyer threatens you with negative feedback.

Starting June 1, 2018, when a buyer leaves less than positive feedback or escalates a Money Back Guarantee claim for one of the above, eBay will automatically remove any negative/neutral feedback. Or so they said. We usually have had to contact eBay and then our experience would depend on the rep. Nonetheless, that is a nice step in the direction of reasonably protecting the reputation of buyers.

Returns

Until it's too late, sellers often don't consider how they will handle returns. Even then, there are subtleties that can minimize the impact on both your reputation and profitability.

Any way you look at it, returns are a challenge.

To begin, understand eBay is a pro-buyer marketplace. Under the terms of the eBay Money Back Guarantee the buyer is protected if "the item didn't arrive, is faulty or damaged or doesn't match the listing." It doesn't matter if the seller has a "no returns" policy.

The two of us once sold a remote control drone for over $200. It was the first item we ever listed with "no returns." It's not the kind of thing we normally sell. With good reason, we were concerned someone would crash it within our 30-day guarantee and want a refund. Within a day of receipt, the buyer filed a return because "I just don't like it." We received negative feedback (which we were able to get removed) but we were not forced to refund their money.

We had a $40 item that was shipped and was lost by the United States Postal System half-way between us and the buyer. We had the tracking details to prove we shipped it and the package was lost at the regional post office near the buyer's location. It didn't matter. The only way you will not have to refund the buyer is if the tracking details show the item as delivered. Despite the lost package situation being no fault of our own, we were forced to refund the buyer's purchase. The good news is we were able to file a claim against the post office and they ultimately refunded the full purchase price along with the postage we paid. It took a few months but they paid.

Item Not as Described

The adage was never truer than at eBay: rush to list an item using a poor description and limited pictures and pay a big price later with returns.

Let's discuss the infamous "not as described" return. To be blunt and perfectly succinct, if the buyer says the item is not as described in any way, eBay will likely hold the seller accountable and force a full refund. That means if you say it's "shiny" and there is one little ½ inch dull spot, they got you. It also means if you say it's 5-1/4 inches and it's actually 5-1/8 inches, they got you. Sure, there are some weasel words about being "significantly" not as described but our experience has been you're going to eat the return. And yes, we place wording in each listing that specs, models, etc. may be vary. It doesn't matter. Not as described is a big opportunity for eBay. It's the sort of issue that can't be compared to Amazon or Walmart. To Amazon and Walmart, a $100 return is not a big deal. To a small eBay seller, a $100 return that was new and cannot be resold could be huge.

Understand when it comes to returns, anything that is not described in full through pictures, the item condition or the item description could be fair game. As noted above, some sellers have argued the item was not "significantly" different and lost. Again, eBay is a pro-buyer marketplace. Take your time and make your listing descriptions the best they can be.

Buyers have also learned if an item is "defective," eBay will automatically approve the return. We had a buyer claim an item was defective because it didn't fit. We had identified the size in the listing in no less than four places. When we asked the buyer (politely) in what way the item didn't fit given the sizes in the listing, they suddenly went quiet and never returned the item. We were able to later have the case closed in our favor.

Even if a seller somehow avoids a return, there can still be negative feedback. Negative feedback can have a much larger financial impact on future sales than the cost of a return. Unfortunately, unless the seller can somehow have it removed, the feedback will be there for the next 12 months.

Set Return Guidelines and Be Positive!

So, what's a seller to do? We offer the following advice:

1) Offer free 30 day returns on all listings. Within the "Returns Policy" state you provide free returns for 30 days **for defective items**. Go on to state you will provide a postage paid return shipping label. For defective items, eBay will hold sellers to this standard anyway. To us, it makes sense to state it and get the "Free Returns" badge on your listings.

2) If an item is defective or the wrong item was shipped, we will generally refund the full purchase price (or send a replacement if we have it). The following positive feedback comments are

from buyers where there was a problem and we quickly treated them the way we would want to be treated. In all cases, a bad situation was turned into positive, sometimes embarrassingly positive, feedback.

- very kind super awesome to work with helps in every way these are good people

- Great Seller went above and beyond to make it right!!!!!

- USPS lost package, no fault of seller

- One book got damaged in transit. Excellent communication led to a quick resolve!

One situation that went from bad to good is when we shipped the wrong item. We received a friendly FYI from the buyer after they had already left positive feedback. They calmly pointed out we sent the wrong item. That very day we shipped via priority mail the correct item along with an apology and a prepaid mailer to return the wrong item. As a result, they wrote the following personal note to us:

> *Thank you for taking the time to provide for your customer. In today's world of instant everything, it's good to be provided with respectable and efficient service.*

They made our day.

3) Even if the return is because the buyer "just didn't like it" get creative and determine how to economically accept the return or issue at least a partial refund while protecting your feedback reputation.

In those cases, we will ask the buyer to kindly go ahead and leave feedback knowing for a full week after receipt from a Top Rated Seller they can only leave positive feedback. It is important to understand it is not kosher to explicitly trade positive feedback for a refund. That's feedback extortion and very much against the rules. With a request for feedback we include an offer for some type of refund or compensation. This increases the possibility of the transaction not negatively affecting your reputation while also providing an out with eBay that you offered a refund and the buyer declined it.

Shipping Costs

It seems like some people guess and others make sure they're covered by charging a penny for the item and $99 for the shipping. Since eBay started including comments regarding shipping in the feedback, the latter practice has all but disappeared. Such a practice is not going to save on fees either as the eBay fee is now based on the selling price *and* the shipping cost. Today, eBay strongly suggests the shipping be free. So, the question becomes how is a seller to appropriately price their items to include shipping?

An easy, comparatively inexpensive way is to purchase a scale and then use the eBay Shipping Calculator (ebay.com/ shp/Calculator). On the first page, enter the details regarding the shipment. For most items, all that is needed is

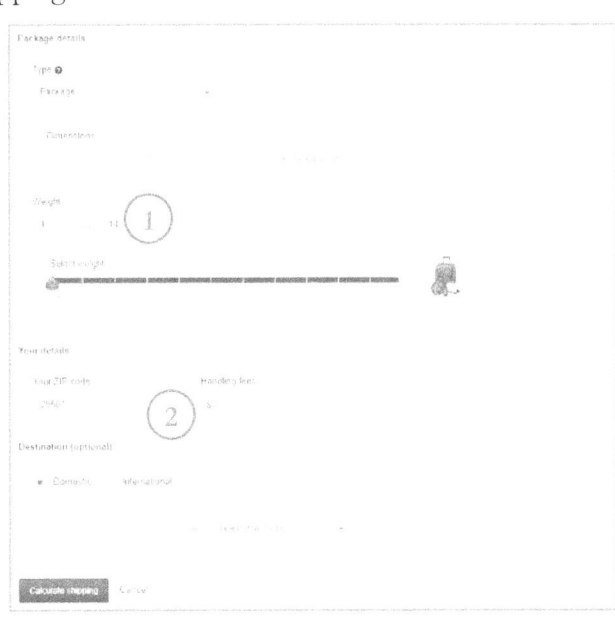

Obtain a shipping cost using the eBay Shipping Calculator by 1) entering the weight and 2) your Zip Code

the weight and your zip code.

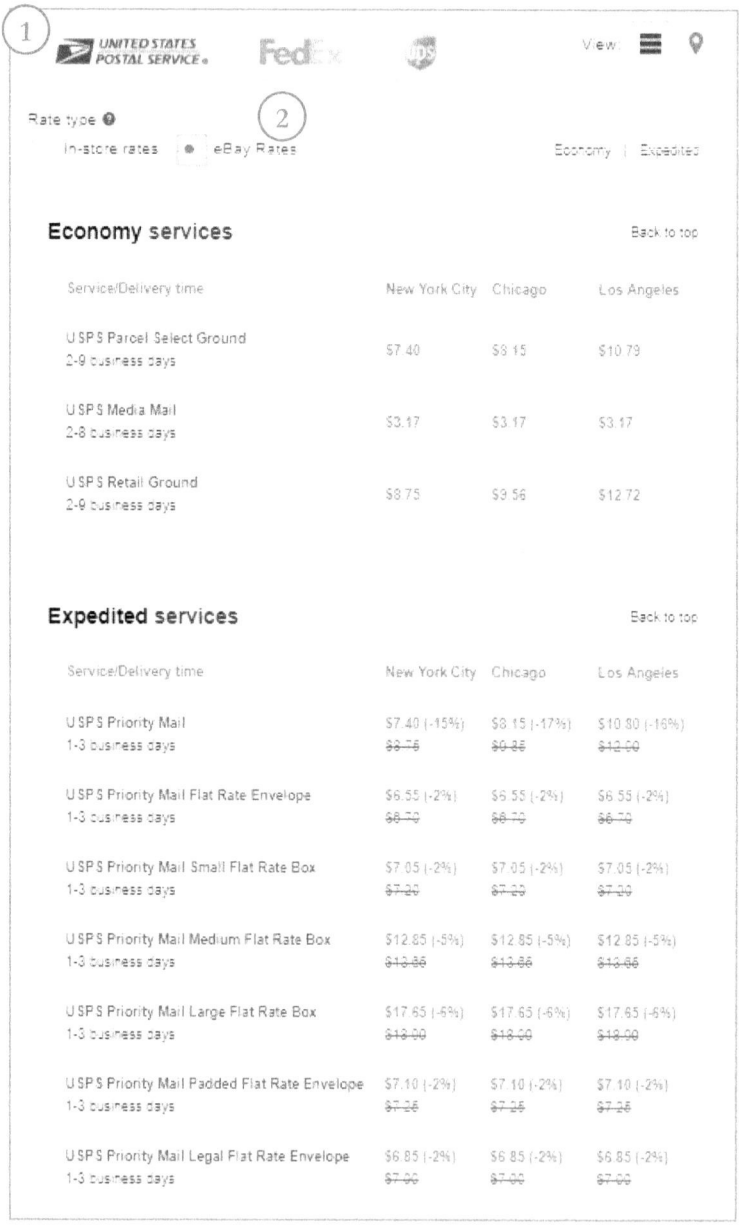

1) Select USPS, FedEx or UPS and 2) click on the eBay Rates button

Most of the time, the USPS shipping costs will be the lowest. Notice the difference between the USPS Media Mail rate and all the others. If an item falls into the media rate, this will always be the lowest option. For additional details on what can be shipped USPS media rate, please refer to Addendum 1.

It is against federal postal regulations to modify, turn inside out, use as packing, or utilize free U.S.P.S supplies for anything other than their intended purpose!

In the preceding illustration a shipping weight of 1 lb. 14 oz. was used. Notice the rate table does not include "First Class." The USPS First Class rate is only available up to 1 lb. (16 oz.). Above 1 lb., USPS priority mail tends to be the least expensive shipping option with flat rate packaging provided by the Post Office as the lowest priority rate cost. By flat rate we're talking about those priority packaging materials (like the padded mailers) that are specifically marked "flat rate." You can order free priority packaging at store.usps.com.

If the item is above 1 lb. and cannot be shipped in flat rate packaging provided by the USPS, shipping can get both expensive and confusing real quick. At this point shipping will likely be made in a package provided by the seller at varying rates provided by USPS, FedEx or UPS.

Selling Limits

Of all eBay's rules, this one was in our way the most. When a seller first begins to sell on eBay, selling limits are placed on how much the seller can list. The thinking is eBay wants to protect new sellers from getting in over their head and then missing shipments, receiving bad feedback, on and on. In theory, it's a good idea and one we initially liked. Initial selling limits were provided for both the quantity of items we could list, as well as, the total value we could list. With our starting emphasis on decluttering items we no longer needed, the provided overall limits seemed reasonable enough.

The problem is selling limits are also present for each category. Unfortunately, a new seller doesn't realize that until they run into them. For us, we were not allowed to list more than 5 music CDs and 5 textbooks. As we had dozens of each, we had a problem. To us, they were ridiculous limits. Either you trust a seller or you don't. If you don't, setting a limit of 5 CDs is not going to stop them from selling pirated music. After all, that kind of activity would tend to show up real quick in the seller's feedback. Similarly, for the textbooks we were given a limit of 5 texts. A limit of 5 would not even allow a student to consistently sell all their books at the end of a semester. What made it even worse is the limits were a total for the month. If a new seller listed 5 CDs in a 7-day auction, the seller could not list another CD for the rest of the month. Did we mention how ridiculous we thought this was? *sigh*

Selling limits is one of the reasons we were forced to call eBay Customer Service. Initially, we had no idea what the non-descript error message meant. During our first call our recollection is they allowed us to go to maybe 10 music CDs. In yet another call, we were able to get them to temporarily allow us to list as many as we could during a 3-day period. Having been burned on the limited-day timeframes, we were forced to list them all good-until-canceled. Once again, it made no sense we be allowed to list a CD good 'til cancelled and it renew automatically but we couldn't list it for 7 or 30 days and then relist it.

Duration ℹ️

Good 'Til Cancelled ▾

Listings renew automatically every 30 days, based on the listing terms at that time, until all quantities sell or the listing ends. Each time a listing renews and when an item sells, you'll be charged applicable fees.

We could list music CDs Good 'Til Cancelled but we couldn't re-list the same CD if we chose a shorter duration.

We know, even as a Top Rated Plus Seller, we still have selling limits. We can see the overall quantity and value limits on Seller Hub (ebay.com/sh/ovw). It seems like within months they allowed us to list several thousand items. The overall limits were never an issue for us despite doing a volume that quickly qualified us as an eBay Top Rated Seller.

Customer Service

Warning: eBay is not customer-centric, buyer or seller. They may not respect your time or your thoughts as to what the issues are. Some may not understand the rules any better than you do. If a frustrating, drawn-out, stressful interaction is anticipated, there's a good chance of success.

Having said that, like so many other things, the quality of eBay Customer Service depends with whom you speak. We have reached customer support agents, domestic and foreign, who were beyond helpful that quickly and efficiently worked the issues. We have also run into steadfast control freaks who seem to make it their goal to make our life as a seller as difficult as possible.

What we have noticed is the customer service agents have a great deal of latitude. If they want, they can help with most anything. We have also noticed there is a difference in the quality of … we'll call it support and friendliness … between eBay call centers. To our knowledge there are call centers in Salt Lake City, Austin, the Philippines and Ireland. There could be more as others have talked of speaking to customer service representatives based in California, India and Bulgaria.

The highest probability of reaching a domestic customer service representative is between 9 AM and 4 PM CST/MST.

It varies but we have had the most success when speaking to eBay Customer Service in a stateside call center (Utah or Texas). The best chance to reach a team based in the U. S. is to call during their normal business hours (i.e., Monday through Friday, 9:00 AM to 4:00 PM CST/MST). Calls outside those hours will likely be diverted to an overseas call center. Regardless of the hour, when there is heavy call volume, expect calls to be diverted overseas.

To reach eBay Customer Service, click on the Help & Contact selection at the bottom of the eBay home screen. The options to speak to eBay via telephone are at the bottom of the resulting page. Expect to be asked numerous questions and offered a variety of online support alternatives. If persistent, one can reach someone on the phone. When you've finally navigated through the maze, you'll be provided a toll-free number and a 7-digit claim number. The claim number is to help with routing to the correct eBay department.

Another option is to call 866-540-3229. This is the number that is normally provided when following the steps outlined in the preceding paragraph. This is much faster on the front end (no maze!) but appreciate there will likely be delays as you explain from the beginning what you need. Expect to be transferred at least once … and to have to explain from the beginning each time. During one 1-hour 36-minute phone call we were transferred six different times … twice back to a department we had already visited. Yes, you read correctly … 1 hour and 36 minutes. During the last year we have had a total of five phone calls to eBay Customer Service that have lasted over an hour.

Asking to speak to a supervisor while on the phone will likely prove fruitless. It has for us. You will probably be told none are available. They will take your name and number and will sometimes (less than 50% of the time) call you back. For us, the callbacks we did receive were at odd hours and from a line with a caller ID that did not identify the call as one from eBay. The best option may be to simply call again at another time (during normal U. S. business hours).

eBay has made email support intentionally difficult. From their perspective, online FAQs then phone support are more efficient. Nonetheless, eBay Customer Service can be reached by emailing customerhelp@ebay.com. Be sure to include your eBay ID and send the message from the email address they have on file.

Finally, for Facebook junkies, the group eBay for Business may provide an alternative to email and the telephone. It's our understanding this team is based in California. Expect a roughly 24-hour delay in their response. eBay for Business also publishes helpful videos.

Understand eBay does not effectively use what is known as "standard work practices." That is, there is no standard, consistent way for handling a given situation. As a result, things as simple and routine as a return are handled in different ways. As stated previously, depending on their mood, experience and willingness to help, the results will vary. It can be downright exasperating dealing with them. Nonetheless, while staying firm in your objective, the nicer and more patient you are, the more likely you are to cajole someone into providing the help you need. Again, they have the power to make most anything happen.

eBay Forums

The eBay community forums may be an alternative to contacting eBay directly. It will almost certainly be quicker and less stressful. eBay monitors the forums and will intervene when there are issues or an out-of-bounds topic but do not expect eBay to directly answer questions. Instead, questions are answered by other sellers who are volunteering on their own time to help.

The forums are great for answering how-to questions like "can I ship software as media mail?" As for tips along the lines of selling more faster and easier … not so much. Again, the community forums are populated by other sellers. Do not expect the competition to make life easier for you at their expense.

YouTube

How to do it easier and less expensive tips can often be found on YouTube (youtube.com). There are several "eBay for Beginners" videos.  Some involve a series of videos or episodes that will walk the viewer through basic to advanced selling on eBay.

The better YouTube eBay videos will usually be heavy on selling additional services. Expect affiliate links to products and services where they receive some form of compensation. Likewise, expect some sort of promotion at the beginning and anything beyond the basics to be available elsewhere for a fee. One way to distinguish helpful videos from the total sales pitches is to look at the number of likes and subscribers.

YouTube quality can also be an issue. One of the early but still popular beginner series was recorded in a 360p resolution. That's great for slow Wi-Fi connections but not at all effective when trying to read some of the text and templates they share. On a smartphone it's too small to read and on a desktop monitor, it's blurred. The same series also begins with an introduction to eBay's Global Shipping Program. The Global Shipping Program is an awesome program we use ourselves but it's not the topic a newbie needs to hear first.

Udemy

Udemy (udemy.com) provides relatively inexpensive content from providers around the world. Some of the courses can normally run as much as a couple hundred dollars but Udemy frequently runs sales where all courses are as low as $9.99.

In addition to insight on how to pack and ship, many of the Udemy courses also discuss sourcing, pricing, listing and managing your ecommerce finances. Generally, you will find the content on Udemy more professional and a better quality than free resources like YouTube. That's to be expected as you're paying for it. Templates and PDF-type downloads are often provided to supplement the Udemy online content.

Growth within eBay

It's about the Numbers!

 If you want to sell more, you have to list more. That might be more items or it might be items with higher prices (and better margins). The important thing to know is the numbers on the front-end should be inline with the expectations on the back-end.

Fortunately, the arithmetic is straightforward. If we sell an item for $25 and it cost us $15 to acquire, list and ship, then our profit would be $10.

Selling Price	$25.00
Expenses	
eBay Listing Fee	0.35
eBay Final Value Fee	2.50
PayPal Fee	1.03
Postage	5.53
Packaging	0.60
Cost fo Purchase	5.00
Profit	$10.00

A spreadsheet with these calculations will likely prove helpful. So, if we want sales of $3000 a month, how many $25 items would we need to sell?

Sales Goal	$3,000
Ave Selling Price	$25
Number of Sales Reqd	120 (Goal/Ave Price)

We divided our sales goal of $3000 by the $25 average selling price to calculate 120 sales per month.

Total Sales is the relatively easy-to-obtain number but it is really profit that is our main interest. If we take the total sales dollars and subtract our expenses, we will get our profit (before taxes).

Total Profit

Sales Goal		$ 3,000
Number of Sales	120	
Ave Cost Per Sale	15	
		_1,800_
Profit		$ 1,200

We could have calculated the same number by taking our 120 sales times our average profit per sale of $10.

We could have also reversed the calculation and started with our profit of $10 and determined how many sales it would take to achieve $1200 in profit (i.e., $1200 profit divided by $10 profit per sale equals 120 sales).

Continuing, if we wanted $5000 in profit each month, we would need to sell 500 items ($5000 in profit divided by $10 profit per sale equals 500 sales).

To grow, it is important to understand your costs. It makes no sense to sell more and lose money. Unfortunately, many sellers do not understand their costs. They are shocked when it costs them over $5 to ship an item from one coast to the other. They are in greater shock at the end of the month when they have had great sales but little money in the bank. That's not the fault of eBay!

When sourcing, many sellers will not touch an item unless they can at least double their money. For these sellers, if they will clear only $10 profit, they will not spend more than $5 on the item. Other sellers look for a multiple of four or five times their investment. For these sellers, they will not spend more than $2.50 on an item in which they will only profit $10. Obviously, this is a personal business decision for each seller that includes how they value their own time.

Clean, Welcoming Listings

Consider your own buying habits. How often do you buy from a listing that has no pictures of the product? If you're like us, you likely don't get a warm fuzzy when there is a single line in the listing description … that is typed in all caps. What you want … and a buyer will find more palatable … is a clean, welcoming and informative listing.

Ideally, each of your listings should contain the following:

- An optimized title,
- At least 3 pictures,

- A detailed description of the item condition,
- The specs section completed as applicable,
- An informative description and
- Your terms regarding shipping, returns and the like.

Pictures taken by a smartphone are fine. There's no need for high-end cameras. The lighting should be adequate but there's no need for fancy lights and backgrounds. Many beginners take pictures during daylight hours in front of an open window. Backgrounds can be as simple as white poster board. Later, an inexpensive lightbox may be helpful as it will allow pictures to be taken night or day. If you want the listing to appear in Google searches, Google prefers plain white backgrounds.

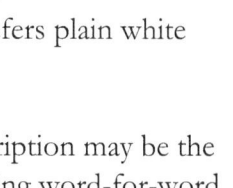

A great source for details to be included in the description may be the manufacturer's packaging. Do not copy the packaging word-for-word as it is likely copyrighted. Specs can also be obtained from the packaging.

Do not neglect including terms in each listing description. For example, if you accept all returns regardless of the reason, state it. On the other hand, if you do not accept returns or returns must be sent back in the same condition sold, that should be stated as well. You might also want to include your payment terms, how and when you normally ship, customs and fee details regarding international purchases and how to contact you for customer service questions. Having these details clarified upfront may be invaluable down the road should issues arise.

Avoid flooding a listing but, in general, the more pictures and specs, the higher the item will likely appear in eBay search results. Obviously, the price, your feedback and your performance as an eBay seller will also impact the search results. But for given feedback and performance levels, the higher search results will tend to have more pictures and specs.

> Little is known about the algorithms used in the eBay search engine Cassini. What is logical, and appears to have little disagreement, is the higher search results tend to have customer-desired features like free shipping, free returns, more pictures, more details and come from sellers with higher performance metrics (e.g., Top Rated Sellers).

Best Offers

Best Offers can be an effective way to sell slow moving items. Essentially, you allow the buyer to make an offer on your item. The option to allow Best Offers can be found in the listing template right below the Price. As desired, limits can be set to automatically accept and decline offers. Once an offer is made, the seller can accept, counter offer or decline.

When a Buy It Now listing allows Best Offers, a "Make Offer" selection will be added below the Buy It Now and Add to Cart buttons.

Price
*Buy It Now price
$

Best Offer
☑ Let buyers make offers. Being flexible with your price may help your item sell faster
☐ Automatically accept offers of at least $
☐ Automatically decline offers lower than $

From the Create Your Listing Template, allow Best Offers by clicking the option right below the Price field

If the offer is accepted, a sale has been made. Depending on your settings, eBay will automatically send the buyer an invoice. Once paid, shipment is made like a normal sale.

Expect to receive offers that are ridiculously low. We have received offers that were so low they did not cover the cost of postage, much less the product cost and any profit. The point is eBay buyers, especially buyers making best offers, are looking for a bargain. Until they ask, they do not know how desperate the seller is. Despite an incredibly low offer, the challenge becomes to respond politely and professionally with a reasonably competitive counter offer. This is especially important on slow moving items. There are exceptions but we usually respond with a counter offer rather than simply declining the offer. When an offer is declined, there is no chance of a sale unless the buyer tries again. When a counter offer is made there is a reasonable probability of a sale.

Did we mention responding politely? ☺ After an absurd offer, resist the urge to kick the person through the virtual goal posts of life. That is easier said than done when considering an offer 25% of the listing price, far below any other listing by other sellers and on a hot item that was listed within the last couple of hours. Such offers will occur!

Instead, a polite and encouraging response might be something along the lines of …

> On this item, this is as low as we want to go. We hope the price meets your approval. Thanks for your offer and interest … have a safe and enjoyable day.

In addition to being polite, one of the things such a response does is it works to eliminate time spent in ongoing negotiations. Most sellers have better things to do than haggle over a few cents. Should there still be some bargaining room on your end, drop the first sentence. Otherwise, if a buyer makes a counter offer to our original counter offer, we usually simply respond with the same price. Unless you are bored and have unlimited time, avoid haggling. After all, the system is called "best offer" for a reason!

If fast and free shipping, free returns or expedited (priority) shipping are included in the listing, point those out in the counter offer. Staying polite, the intent is to be encouraging and competitive while pointing out the advantages of your item versus others.

As for being competitive, a bit of quick market research is likely in order. It is a dynamic marketplace and chances are competitor pricing has changed since the item was originally listed. This means the process used to originally price the item should be repeated. That may mean a quick comparison of other offers including listings on other sites like Amazon. Consideration should also be made regarding the original purchase price of the item and how long it has been listed.

Power Seller Tip	Accepting Best Offers

Before accepting a Best Offer, check the buyer's feedback. If they leave a lot of negative feedback, you might consider passing on the offer.

Sending Offers

In addition to receiving Best Offers, eBay sellers also have the option to send offers to watchers of a listing. There are limits as to how many and how often an offer can be sent. Understand many watchers may not be active buyers but sellers listing comparable items. There's also the risk of irritating a potential buyer with what they might consider to be spam.

Your Own eBay Store

There will come a time when 50 free
listings a month may no longer sufficient.
If you're looking to earn $3000 or more a
month, that time will come sooner rather
than later. There are also benefits such as
free eBay branded shipping materials, a
discount on final value fees and the ability
to put your listings on "vacation" when
you're out of town.

As a demonstration of the potential fee savings, eBay's premium store
owners currently receive a 10% discount on most final fee categories.
Enterprise store owners receive up to a 60% discount on final fees.

A store also allows a seller to email buyers with routine specials.
Newsletters are also a possibility. It's also possible to direct followers
from offsite social media platforms like Instagram and Twitter to your
store. The URL for your store might also be added to your business
card.

There are five levels of eBay stores: Starter, Basic, Premium, Anchor
and Enterprise. A comparison of features and costs at the time of
publication can be found on the facing page.

	Starter	Basic	Premium	Anchor	Enterprise
Yearly subscrip- tion	$4.95/ mo	$21.95/ mo	$59.95/ mo	$299.95/ mo	$2995.95/ mo
Free fixed price inser- tions	100/mo	250/mo	1000/mo	10,000/ mo	100,000/ mo
Vacation Hold	✓	✓	✓	✓	✓
Selling Manager Pro	$15.99/ mo	$15.99/ mo	✓	✓	✓
Terapeak	$19.00/ mo	✓	✓	✓	✓
Best for sellers who …	List up to 100 items per month	List at least 250 items per month	List at least 1000 items per month	List at least 10k items per month and want additional support	List at least 100k items per month and want additional support

Additional details about eBay store subscriptions can be found at ebay.com/help/selling/ebay-stores/ebay-stores.

Title Optimization

To become a successful seller, buyers must first see your listings. Somehow, some way a top seller must stand out. That begins with the item title and details. As a prospective buyer searches for an item, these titles and details are searched for matches. The more encompassing the title and details, the greater the likelihood a listing will be seen.

When it comes to titles, seldom do we accept the default title generated by the eBay catalog when we enter a UPC or ISBN. Instead, we use the title to accurately describe the essence of our product, as well as, to hopefully convey a bit of trust. We also use keywords rather than adjectives. Buyers search for an "automatic coffee maker" and not a "cute coffee maker that will get you going bright and cheerful!" It's also a good idea to spell out words. For example, use New York rather than NY.

To most search engines, the first words in a title tend to be the most important. We begin with the brand followed by the item model or style. If there is room, we continue with sizes and colors. If there is still room, we might add NWT (for New with Tags) for clothing and possibly something like Free Shipping at the very end. Usually, we fill the title and don't have room for extras like the condition or comments about our shipping.

In the case of media, we'll list the book, DVD or CD title followed by the author, star or singer. If it's a music CD and there's room, we'll include the top hits from the CD.

Should images be included in your listing description text, use the alt tag attribute to add relevant keywords. Keywords and headers might also be bolded. We do not know how eBay's Cassini search engine prioritizes but both the alt tag and bold letters receive special attention with other search engines. We also know Google, in particular, prefers images with white backgrounds.

Be cautious when specifying colors. People don't see colors the same. As a matter of fact, the same person doesn't see a given color the same before and after their first coffee ... seriously! There is also a big gap between mobile displays, computer monitors and true colors. Unless the color is so obvious no one could argue, we leave the color out of our descriptions. We'll include it in our pictures but not in words. Let the buyer decide if it's black or a dark navy blue!

Selling Around the World

Selling internationally can dramatically increase the number of potential buyers viewing your listings. What with all the international customs forms and shipping regulations, selling internationally can also dramatically increase the number of headaches and hassle factor associated with selling on eBay.

The good news is eBay has created a service called the Global Shipping Program that has removed most of the headaches and hassles when selling overseas. Essentially, you ship to eBay's distribution system in Kentucky and they handle everything, including customs, import fees and the required paperwork. It couldn't be easier.

ISBN and UPC Codes

The use of ISBN and UPC codes should be straightforward. Both codes are converted into a bar code found on packaging or the back cover of media. ISBN is an acronym for International Standard Book Number and UPC stands for Universal Product Code.

ISBNs are used to identify specific books and UPCs are used to precisely identify other products. In theory, no two books or products should have the same ISBN or UPC number. Matter of fact, versions of the same book (i.e., different editions or the hardcover version versus the paperback or audio book versions) will have different ISBNs. On the surface, it's an effective way to identify a specific version of book or product from all others.

And then there's the real world. Unscrupulous sellers will list an older edition of a book under the new edition's ISBN. When you find something like that, simply report it to eBay. There will be a "Report Item" selection typically before the description on each listing.

There will be a "Report Item" button between the details at the top of a listing and the beginning of the listing description.

Even more rampant is the use of a single UPC number for variations of the same type of product. An unscrupulous seller will identify a hot selling product and list other products under the same UPC. From our experience, the worst areas for this are DVDs and video games. Again, report it to eBay.

Understand, by reporting unscrupulous tactics we're not trying to be the police or "Captains of the World." Like most, we were taught not to rat on people ... except when it comes to safety and costing others. These practices cost other sellers, cost buyers and are disrespectful to the buyer's time to sift through it all to find what they want. From our perspective, there's not a lot of difference between these sellers and sellers offering counterfeit goods.

Another misuse of ISBN and UPC numbers is to not use them at all. As we will explain in a moment, there is a difference in how ISBN and UPC numbers are used. We will discuss UPC numbers first and then ISBN. To begin, appreciate other sellers are the predominant users of UPC numbers. We will say that again as it's important: other sellers are the predominate users of UPC numbers. Let us explain.

Consider your own approach when searching online. Usually, you search for the name of the product or perhaps its manufacturer and model number. The average eBay buyer is no different. They often do not know the UPC or have the product with its bar code in front of them.

A seller on the other hand will typically scan bar codes while sourcing for items and then use the bar code when pricing the item against existing listings. Again, sellers are the predominant users of UPC bar codes. So, to reduce the field of competition, some sellers used to list items without UPC numbers. The  average (read beginning) seller will not see their item (and its price) but buyers will when they search using names, manufacturers and model numbers. Although this practice is perhaps not against any rules, understand eBay wants all sellers to use valid UPC numbers when available. It's also to your advantage as a seller given your items might then appear in offsite (i.e., Google) searches. That can be huge when the item is difficult to find and there aren't many sellers. When available, Manufacturer Part Numbers (MPNs) should also be used.

As alluded earlier, ISBN numbers are used differently. Buyers will search for books using an ISBN. It's often easier to copy and paste an ISBN than a long book title. From search engines like Google, they will also enter an ISBN to compare pricing between eBay and other online venues like Amazon. Especially if a book is one of a very few in existence, a valid ISBN should be used. In this way, if a book listing is a Best Match or one of few in circulation, sales can be generated directly from offsite search engines. We have personally generated a lot of sales this way.

The eBay landscape is changing with respect to UPC and ISBN bar codes. With the advent of the eBay catalog, the appropriate UPC and ISBN are now required. Items not in the catalog are said to be showing up lower in the search results.

Becoming a Top-Rated Seller

To quote eBay, Top Rated and Top Rated Plus Sellers provide "a great experience for their buyers." Top Rated Plus Sellers provide outstanding customer service along with free shipping and a gracious return policy. Listings for Top Rated Sellers will display a special eBay badge.

Listings for a Top Rated Plus Seller will contain a special badge and highlight premium services like Fast 'n Free Shipping and Free Returns.

In addition to the distinctive badging, eBay's Top-Rated Sellers also receive a 10% discount on final fees. Instead of the nominal 10% fee, Top Rated Sellers are charged 9%. Every little bit helps!

The current requirements for becoming a U. S.-based Top Rated Seller include the following:

- Fully comply with eBay's selling practices policy (www.ebay.com/help/policies/selling-policies/selling-practices-policy?id=4346) and have an eBay account that has been active for at least 90 days,
- Have at least 100 transactions and at least $1000 in U. S. sales during the last 12 months,
- Have a defect rate less than 0.5% of all transactions (or a maximum of 3 unique buyers),
- Have less than 0.3% (or a maximum of 2) of cases closed by eBay without seller resolution, and
- Less than 3% (or a maximum of 6) late shipments.

Similarly, a U. S. seller can become a Top Rated Global Seller by having at least 100 transactions and over $1000 in sales to locations outside the United States.

As a side note, the Fast 'n Free designation in the last illustration is because 1) both the seller and buyer reside in the lower 48 U. S. states, 2) based on the seller's stated handling time, delivery will be a maximum of four business days, and 3) free shipping is the default shipping option in the listing.

Hands-On Learning

A Definition and a Bit of Background

From his days in the business world, Mike learned and practiced a system of hands-on learning called *kaizen* (pronounced kye-zen). It's part of the Lean toolset used by many organizations like Toyota, General Electric, the Environmental Protection Agency (EPA) and the United States military. Some refer to the application of kaizen in the retail marketplace as Lean Retail.

Kaizen is a Japanese word. It literally translates as "excellent change." Some people, like Toyota, keep it simple and refer to kaizen as continuous improvement.

Kaizen: Excellent Change

Fundamentally, kaizen is a team-based activity of hands-on problem solving with a heavy dose of deep respect for all you encounter. As a result, changes made through kaizen tend to be win-win-win ... a win for the business, a win for the customer and a win for the employees involved. If a change is not win-win-win, then it is not an "excellent change" and more work is encouraged.

So, the obvious question becomes how do you use kaizen when selling on eBay? Going back to our earlier definition, kaizen helps solve problems. As a problem arose, we used kaizen … hands-on learning … to resolve the problem. From how to package something to dealing with returns, kaizen has made our job as a reseller easier and more enjoyable. The process has also resulted in some embarrassingly complimentary feedback. Kaizen is simple to do and best of all it works.

Using Kaizen to Solve Problems: Packaging

Early on, we did like most new sellers and grabbed an empty shipping box laying around the house. Combined with our initial inability to use inexpensive packaging tape, our boxes looked awful. It wasn't something we were proud of and was really the first issue we attempted to work using kaizen.

We began by gathering data … what kind of products were we listing? What were some of the packaging options available? How did the best in the business (like Amazon) handle the issue? We began to answer these kinds of questions to begin our learning journey. Until that time, we had no working knowledge about options like white poly mailers, air pillows or air-jacketed mailers.

After obtaining a number of samples, we started our hands-on learning in earnest. We learned what kind of products could ship in a mailer versus a heavier, more expensive box. We also experimented with how to place our items in the packaging to first protect the item while also minimizing the overall weight. Creative placement of the folded packing slip and label were one of our breakthroughs. By having lighter items, we were then able to become even more competitive with our pricing. It was also a good feeling when customers started recognizing our packaging upgrades in their feedback … good stuff for sure!

Using Kaizen to Solve Problems: Returns

The two of us were caught off guard by our first return. We felt we had done nothing wrong, yet we were being forced to accept the return. Again, we started learning. Some of the Facebook groups were instrumental in sharing the return steps and what options we had. We made it through the first return with minimal damage but knew we had to find a better, less stressful way. Our better way thinking began with how do we minimize returns from the start? Likewise, when a return does occur, what can we do to minimize the damage to both our finances and our feedback reputation?

As we started to problem solve, we realized we were going to be forced to accept defective items and items we didn't do a good job describing. That's when we started offering free 30 day returns for "defective" items. We clearly stated in each listing we would happily pay for the return of defective items. We stressed defective. As returns have occurred since we took this step, we've been able to avoid most buyer-remorse "I just don't like it" returns.

Another finding was the quality and accuracy of our listing descriptions was not where we wanted it to be. Today, after our learning, we spend more time than most on our pictures, specs and the description wording. So, turn it around. When you're a buyer, do you find a professional looking listing with quality photographs, detailed specs and a graphic description better than the listing with the default photos and all cap description that essentially says, "buy me at your own risk?" Exactly … LOL.

It's true it takes us longer to produce a listing. That's a downside. On the plus side, our listings look professional and appealing. That in turn has resulted in more business, higher prices and better feedback.

How to Kaizen Problem Solve

So, how do you kaizen problem solve? Good question.

We suggest starting with the fundamentals. That means defining what a problem is to your business. For us, we kept it simple. A problem to the two of us is having an idea or goal that is not implemented. Our other problems are just like other sellers: returns, delayed shipping, lost packages, defective products, etc. We then follow four steps ...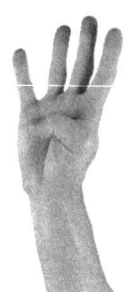

1) Clearly identify the challenge and the expectations not being met. Someone not involved in the problem should easily be able to grasp why the issue is important. You don't have to reduce your thoughts to paper but it may help.

2) Gather data. What we want is to understand "how it really is" versus "what we think it is" or "what it should be." We're after reality and not beliefs.

3) Begin to experiment. Ideally, this is hands-on but it could also be an open verbal discussion with you and a confidant. That discussion might go something like "if we do this, how will that affect the customer? Will it be respectful and better for them? Will it be win-win-win for us, the customer and our partners like eBay and USPS?"

4) Repeat the process ... continuously. There's a reason it's called continuous improvement. It's not necessary to solve all the world's problems at once. Matter of fact, the 80/20 rule works very well in eCommerce. If we can spend 20% of the effort and get 80% of the benefits, then let's do it understanding if we're truly doing continuous improvement, we'll be back.

Other Uses of Kaizen

We have also used kaizen for our inventory management system layout and labeling, our shipping area layout and even what we say on our packing slips. The potential applications are endless. If there is a problem, a potential problem or a goal we haven't achieved, it's prime for kaizen.

Our experience with kaizen learning indicates we do not need to be the lowest price. Our Top Rated Seller, Fast and Free Shipping, Free Returns and professional looking listings allow us to charge a bit more. It works and you should try kaizen problem-solving to help you achieve the same!

Tracking Your Inventory

Necessary Evil

To put the challenge in perspective, tracking your inventory is a pain. Not tracking your inventory is an absolute nightmare. If the nightmare goes on long enough, eBay will place you in a special group of sellers where you pay a penalty of 4% in addition to the normal  final value fee. We understand they do that right before they boot you. And no, you don't get a special badge.

Seriously, if you value your time, you will spend less time overall having a good inventory management system versus not having one and always having to search for items.

Spreadsheets

Based on conversations with other sellers, it appears most use some type of spreadsheet. Microsoft Excel tends to be one of the more popular but there's also Google Sheets and Open Office (which are both free).

The inventory management spreadsheet is ideally integrated with your pricing. A simple spreadsheet might look like the following:

| Item | Date Acq'd | Source | Cost | Storage Location | | Weight | Shipping Cost | Selling Price | eBay Fees | PayPal Fees | Pkg Cost | Total Cost to Sell | Profit |
				Area/Shelf	Bin/No.								
iPhone 6S	6-May	Garage Sale	50.00	S2	03	0.5 lb	4.33	160.00	16.00	4.94	0.40	75.67	84.33

Note the storage location usually has two components: an area or shelf and a bin or item number. Suppose you were selling clothes and stored them in plastic totes. Perhaps you could get 40 to 50 pieces of clothing in each tote. When the first tote is full, you will need to start putting the clothes in a second tote. To help determine which tote was used, it will be necessary to number the totes ... easy enough.

Now imagine you have a tote full of 40 to 50 pieces of clothing. Do you really want to sort through all the pieces looking for a particular one? Of course not. That is the reason you want to number each item. If you then stack the items in numerical order within each tote, searching becomes a piece of cake.

We use a combination of storage racks, plastic totes and zipper-closure bags. The important thing is to consider not only how you're going to store an item but also how you're going to easily find it when it sells! Additional details and some of our thinking (and pitfalls) regarding storage can be found in the next chapter.

Add-Ons

There are software packages that track inventory, as well as, help list faster and more professionally. Some are standalone and some integrate with conventional spreadsheets like Microsoft Excel.

The more popular packages tend to be Inkfrog, Sellbrite, Channel Advisor and Auctiva. Most include professional listing templates and some integrate with multiple platforms. For example, if an item sells that is listed on both Amazon and eBay, the software will automatically update the listed inventory on the other platform.

QuickBooks

We use QuickBooks but not its inventory management system. For us, QuickBooks is just too complicated and time consuming compared to a spreadsheet. We had also already set up the spreadsheet and would have had to redo everything had we switched. The spreadsheet also had another big advantage as it was used for pricing.

There are a number of YouTube videos that explain how to use QuickBooks inventory management.

Numbering

Before we leave the topic of inventory management, we should discuss the various ways to number items and their storage containers/racks. Most sellers assign a number to items that do not have a unique UPC or ISBN bar code. Pre-owned clothing is a good example. Clothing might be numbered something like C0001, C0002, C0003, etc. The "C" indicates it is clothing and the 4 digits would allow up to 9999 distinct pieces of clothing.

Another way to number items is to use the manufacturer's numbers. For example, if you were selling sports cards, you might label a particular card 2006 Topps Baseball #125 or 06TBB125 for short. You could then store and group all the 2006 Topps Baseball cards in the same box or tray. Label the container on the outside and you're good to go.

Speaking of containers … they also need to be numbered. As discussed in the earlier clothing illustration, whether it's bins of clothes or boxes of sports cards, chances are good there will be more than one container. To keep from having to search through everything, number the containers. In addition to the number of the container, we also place the numbers of the items found inside. Again, if we were storing clothes, the first bin might have a label that indicated it was Bin 01 with items C0001-C0040 inside.

So, what do you do when you sell half the items in the bin? What we do is consolidate two bins into one. Continuing with the clothes illustration, if we sold 20 pieces from Bin 01 containing C0001 to C0040 and another 20 pieces from Bin 02 containing C0041 to C0080, we would combine the two totes and label it Bin 01 (C0001 to C0080). We then use the empty tote to store new items. The only downside is pulling a container leaves a hole in the numbering. For us, the hole is preferable to going out and acquiring more storage space. As long as we leave the containers in order, the holes become a non-issue.

That's how we track our inventory. In the next chapter, we'll dive deeper into inventory storage.

Storing Your Inventory

Prep before you Store!

It's a good practice to clean and prep your items before taking pictures and storing them. You probably don't want to take a picture of dirty athletic shoes. You also don't want to leave price stickers on merchandise. A bit of cleaning and prepping is necessary before continuing.

Power Seller Tip | For items with price stickers, we use a product called an adhesive removal product and then a label removal tool. Two of the  more popular are Goo Gone and Scotty Peeler. We prefer plastic removal tools as the metal tools have a greater potential to dig into and scratch the product.

We provide a quick brushing and polish for shoes. For boots and athletic shoes, use something like a Waterpik to quickly remove dirt. It's also a good idea to spray with a foot odor spray. Yes, we usually wear disposable gloves when handling shoes.

We launder pre-owned "clean" clothing on a special dryer setting that freshens the material and removes any musty smells. We also add a dryer anti-static sheet like Bounce. For new clothes, we might steam them or use a product like Downy Wrinkle Releaser. Small amounts of pilling can also be removed with a handheld fuzz removal tool. To preserve the freshness, clothing is then sealed in a plastic bag. You might ask why not hang the clothes? There are two reasons. The first is they take more space when they are hung. The second is we fold them anyway to ship them. So, why not save space and time and fold the clothes now? Exactly …

Only after your items have been prepped are they ready to be photographed.

Photographing Your Items

There's no need for high-end photography equipment or a fancy camera. A good smartphone camera is more than adequate. Lights are not necessary as long as you're able to provide adequate lighting with minimal shadows. Many beginning sellers take their pictures in front of a window.

So we might take pictures when we don't have adequate daylight, we use a lightbox we bought on eBay. We already had two photography lights we placed on each side.

As for a background, Google suggests plain white. As a result, we use white backgrounds on anything with a UPC or ISBN that might be found by Google. One one-of-a-kind items like pre-owned clothing that is not likely to be found by Google, we use a color background. We also use a color background when photographing clear glass items.

eBay allows up to 12 photographs per listing. We come close on clothing but otherwise usually have 3 or 4 pictures. For example on a book or DVD, we will have the front, the back and an expanded shot of any descriptive information.

Planning Your Inventory Layout

Benjamin Franklin's adage "failing to plan is planning to fail" is alive and well in twenty-first century eBay ecommerce.

When we started, we didn't give much thought to how to store and organize our inventory. As our initial goal was only 50 items, how bad could it be? Well, it was bad enough we had to cancel an order when we couldn't find the item. It also took us way too long to search through our piles that were stashed here and there around the house.

Having a plan from the beginning will save time and effort.

That didn't last long. We're much too lazy to have to search for things. So, we dedicated two bookcases in an upstairs hallway to the effort. We were able to organize like items on the bookcases and there was no more searching throughout the house. Along about 100 items we outgrew the bookcases. It was at that point we decided we needed a real plan.

Our children are grown and out of the house so the plan became to convert an empty bedroom into a storage area. We also put a shipping table and photography lightbox in the same room. Depending on the type of items being sold (and the local heat and humidity), a corner in a garage might work better than an unused room. The point is to somehow dedicate space to the effort.

We talked together about an approach with the unused bedroom and called ourselves planning. A drawing with rough dimensions will go a long way. It wasn't until we sketched a layout on a piece of paper that the ideas truly started flowing. That was when we came up with the idea of the shipping table and lightbox. With a bit of forethought, we 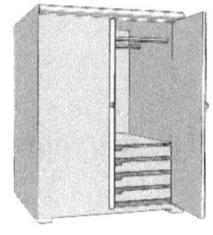 were also able to arrange the room in a way to allow future growth. Your mileage may vary depending on what you sell but we were able to list well over a thousand items with just one room and some hallway bookcases.

Labeling

If the containers are numbered, you may not need a label on each item. It depends on their size, quantity, etc. Just do what makes sense.

The one place you may want to label is clothing, whether you think you need it or not. Once you get into it, you may have quite a few "Joseph A Banks Blue XL Dress Shirts." For that reason, we always number clothing. In addition to the C0001-type numbers discussed in the last chapter, we also add the last 4 digits of the eBay item number. Right up there with not being able to find a shirt is sending the wrong shirt. As something of a mistake-proofing check, we use both numbers for verification.

Containers

In general, we use the least expensive container readily available that will allow us to use labels and other visuals to quickly find an item. Searching is not high on our list of fun things we like to do together.

Sometimes, like in the case of clothing, it's a thin plastic bag. Those items of clothing are then placed in a larger tote. We use clear totes so we can see inside.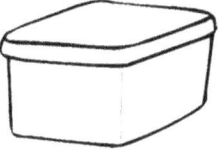

Cardboard boxes work great for many heavy items like tools. We will often remove the aisle-facing side of the box so we can again see inside.

Books and other electronic media like DVDs, Blu-Ray discs, music CDs, software and audiobooks are stored in bookcases. We alphabetize everything but the books.

Bookcases and Other Shelving

In our opinion, bookcases remain the best option for books. As we said earlier, we have also used bookcases for media like DVDs and music CDs. For books, we adjust the distance between shelves based on the height of the book. For that reason, we prefer bookcases with adjustable shelving. Tall books stay together on a shelf and short books are together on another shelf. This saves overall shelf space.

As for DVDs, Blu-Rays, music CDs, software and audiobooks, we alphabetize them. Alphabetizing takes a few minutes initially but locating sold items becomes a breeze.

Bookcases are fine for books and electronic media but don't work nearly as well for heavy objects like tools. Economical industrial-grade racks can be found at the warehouse stores and big box hardware stores. Shelves capable of supporting several hundred pounds can be purchased for around $100. We prefer shelves that are 72 inches tall, 48 inches wide and 24 inches deep. They're a tad more expensive but they will also comfortably hold two totes per shelf. We also prefer shelves without holes. If you're halfway handy, sturdy storage shelves can be easily built out of 2x4s and ¾" plywood. Sand the shelves and completely sink the nails and screws but there's no need for anything fancy.

Extra Rooms and the Garage

Before considering outside warehouse space, revisit and optimize your current situation. A bit of upfront thought could save thousands in rent. Understand it's not just space but also electricity, Wi-Fi and air conditioning that must be considered. For that reason, many sellers reconsolidate within their home.

Sometimes, that reconsolidation involves taking over a spare room like we did. Other times, it might mean part of the workshop, garage or a shed in the backyard. Keep in mind window air conditioners and space heaters in a garage or shed tend to be a lot less expensive than renting a warehouse.

Managing Your Finances

Another Necessary Evil

If you thought inventory management was a pain, it's nothing compared to the hassle of managing your finances. The bottom line is you don't have to watch your finances. Of course, you might lose your shirt, your business and your home in the process. The choice is sometimes pretty clear. Either manage your finances or don't eat. Well, there's a third choice: go back to a normal job working for someone else.

Watching Your Costs

To manage your finances, it's necessary to watch your costs. By watching your costs, we mean capturing all of them. The key word in the last sentence is "all." You don't have to watch "all" the costs but then you're not going to be able to deduct them on your taxes. You're also not going to know your true selling costs.

An example is the trip to the post office. Most people do not go to the local post office every day. Instead, they use e-mail and an online bill pay system. If you're a decent eBay seller, you will go to the post office at least once a day. The mileage to the post office can be a business expense. It can't be written off though if it's not tracked.

That trip to the post office is also part of the cost of selling an item and should be incorporated into your pricing. As we demonstrate in the illustration that follows, those costs can add up. If we travel to a post office that is 5 miles away six days a week, our costs might be something like the following:

Roundtrip distance to Post Office	2 x 5 miles = 10 miles
Trips per Week	x 6 trips/week
Weeks in a Year	x 50[1] weeks/year
Current IRS Mileage Allowance	x $0.58/mile
	$1740 total annual cost

That's a business deduction of $1740 per year. For most eBay beginners, that's significant. If it's not significant to you, we'll send you our PayPal address and you can start sending your extra money our way. Yes, the two of us are available for adoption. ☺

Carrying the arithmetic to the item level … let's assume we average 10 sales a day.

Cost of Trips to the Post Office	$1740 per year
Weeks in a Year	÷ 50[1] weeks/year
Trips per Week	÷ 6 trips/week
Sales per Day	÷ 10 sales/day
	$0.58 per item sold

Those calculations tell us if you sold 10 items a day and your post office is 5 miles away, trips to the post office are costing you $0.58 an item. Those costs are real. The cost of gas and wear on your car are real. The only way to account for them in the eyes of the IRS is to track them.

---

[1] As there are 52 weeks in the year, we're being conservative by using 50. This accounts for federal holidays and the fact some days we may not have any sales.

A couple of disclaimers are in order. We're not CPAs or tax code experts. We don't know if you can claim a business expense for trips to the post office or not. You should consult a qualified tax professional before claiming this or any other business expense on your taxes.

Likewise, some will argue packages can be picked up by your local mail carrier. If that happens, there's no need for the trip to the post office. Our experience is residential mail carriers do not have a good track record in scanning packages. It's not normal to scan as, at best, they're handling routine letters. If it's not scanned until later (often the next morning as it has arrived at the post office at the end of the day), you'll be dinged by eBay if you've opted for one day handling.

Space in your mailbox and the mail carrier's vehicle may also be an issue. If you're shipping 10 packages a day, that could overwhelm your mailbox and consume a large portion of the carrier's available space. Warm chocolate chip cookies may help but sooner or later your carrier will tire of picking up all your packages. And if you live in a subdivision, there may be rules against running a business out of your home. In such a situation, the less attention you draw, the better.

Other Business Expenses

Again, we're not tax professionals. Before acting on any of the information in this chapter, please consult a qualified tax professional.

In addition to mileage, you may be able to claim business expense deductions for the following:

- Interest on business loans,
- Professional fees to accountants and attorneys,
- Office supplies and postage,
- Rental costs for leased equipment,
- Repairs and maintenance for business-related equipment,
- Taxes and licenses,
- Some overnight lodging and travel,
- Some business-related meals,
- Some utility expenses and
- Wages and fringe benefits paid to your employees.

The list goes on. For example, you may be able to deduct that portion of your home used by your business. As before, this and the other ideas we've shared should be validated by a tax professional.

PayPal

PayPal is an online payment system that provides an electronic alternative to checks and money orders. It's roots began in 1998 and it became a wholly owned subsidiary of eBay in  2002. From 2002 to the present, it's been the primary payment method for eBay. At the strong encouragement of Carl Icahn, eBay spun off PayPal in 2015. Within eBay's new managed payments initiative, PayPal will be one of many payment options offered by eBay. Other payment options will include the normal credit cards along with Apple Pay and Google Pay.

The reason we mention it here is PayPal or something like it may be an option for tracking your expenses. If your major purchases are made through PayPal or a PayPal debit/credit card, your statements will go a long way in terms of helping you watch your expenses. Again, we mention PayPal only because it is currently so integrated with eBay.

Down the road (when eBay's Managed Payments are fully implemented), any dedicated credit card or mobile pay system could serve the same purpose.

Spreadsheets

We're back to our infamous spreadsheets. Like before, you may choose to use Microsoft Excel or any of the free tools like Google Sheets or Open Office.

If you go the spreadsheet route, we suggest building an expense section into the same workbook used for your inventory management and pricing. As an expenditure occurs, capture it in the proper expense category. At the end of the year, you have everything in one tidy place for your income taxes. Your expenses may vary (did we say consult a financial professional? ☺) but your spreadsheet may look something like the following:

		Total MTD Expense	$ 307.14		Total MTD Profit
					$ 1,286.19
Date	Expenditure	Category	Amount		
1-May	Toner	Supplies	50.00		
1-May	Shipping labels	Supplies	15.00		
3-May	UPS Store box rental	Dues/Subscriptions	120.00		
5-May	State Sales Taxes	Taxes and Fees	22.19		
7-May	Internet Service	Dues/Subscriptions	40.00		
15-May	eBay Store	Dues/Subscriptions	59.95		

By having your expenses and your costs for resale items in the same spreadsheet, it's possible to calculate your month-to-date and year-to-date profit. Like a scale in the bathroom, these numbers provide helpful insight how your business is performing relative to expectations.

Freeware

Wave (waveapps.com) is a free software package for small businesses. In their words: "When we say free, we mean it. No set-up fees, no hidden charges. Not a free trial. Not a free limited version. Free means free." The base software will perform the basic invoicing, accounting and receipt scanning required for a small business to function.

At the time of publication, Wave had 165 employees. So, what's the catch? How do they make money? Wave charges for additional financial services like credit card processing, bank payment processing and payroll. Even then, the fees for those services tend to be competitive. Their credit card processing fees are on par with PayPal, if not a little less.

With Wave, do not expect many frills. The software is functional and can be a great platform, especially for startups. To begin, it is web-based. All you need is a connection to the internet. For mobile invoicing and receipt scanning there are apps for both iOS and Android. Email support is available to everyone. Live chat support is provided for their paid financial services.

QuickBooks

The most popular small business accounting package is QuickBooks. QuickBooks is available in a desktop version that retails for about $300. The mobile version comes in 3 subscription models that start at $20 per month. The most popular mobile plan is $35 per month and includes the ability to track inventory by as many as 5 users. The desktop version also has the capability to track inventory.

If you use QuickBooks, transfers to your accountant are easier. Your accountant is also more prone to love you. ☺

Addendums

The following addendums provide additional details and insight to some key topics. A conscious effort was made to keep the chapters short and uncluttered. This information is provided for those who want a bit more detail.

Addendums

Addendum 1

Media Mail Service[2]

Addendum 1 – USPS Media Mail
Media Mail® service has special eligibility requirements for permissible contents. Media Mail rates are limited to the items listed below:

- Books (at least 8 pages).
- Sound recordings and video recordings, such as CDs and DVDs.
- Playscripts and manuscripts for books, periodicals, and music.
- Printed music.
- Computer-readable media containing prerecorded information and guides or scripts prepared solely for use with such media.
- Sixteen millimeter or narrower width films.
- Printed objective test materials and their accessories.
- Printed educational reference charts.
- Loose-leaf pages and their binders consisting of medical information for distribution to doctors, hospitals, medical schools, and medical students.

Media Mail Packages may not contain advertising except that books may contain incidental announcements of other books and sound recordings may contain incidental announcements of other sound recordings. In accordance with standards in the Mailing Standards of the United States Postal Service, Domestic Mail Manual (DMM 300) 173.3.2, Media Mail Packages are subject to inspection by the Postal Service™. Upon such inspection, matter not eligible for the Media Mail rate may be assessed at the proper rate and sent to the recipient postage due, or the sender may be contacted for additional postage (DMM 604.8.1).

---

[2] From the United States Postal Service (USPS) website
http://about.usps.com/notices/not121/not121.htm

For more information about Media Mail service, please visit www.usps.com or call 1-800-ASK-USPS (1-800-275-8777). Complete explanations of qualified items may be found in DMM 173.3.2.

Notice 121
July 2008
PSN 7610-07-000-4037

Addendum 2

Proper Use of USPS Priority Flat Rate Containers

The following is from the USPS website[3]. It was initially part of an internal bulletin to USPS employees.

DMM Notice: Proper Use of Flat Rate Containers

Employees are reminded of the proper use of Priority Mail Express® and Priority Mail® Flat Rate envelopes and boxes (containers).

According to Mailing Standards of the United States Postal Service, Domestic Mail Manual (DMM®), when sealing a Flat Rate Envelope (FRE) or Flat Rate Box (FRB), the container flaps must be able to close within the normal folds. Tape may be applied to the flaps and seams to reinforce the container, provided the design of the container is not enlarged by opening the sides and the container is not reconstructed in any way. The weight restriction for domestic Flat Rate Envelopes and Boxes is 70 lbs.

If an FRE or FRB is presented at the office of mailing and the customer has manipulated or reconstructed it, the container is accepted using weight and zone — not the Flat Rate price. A customer is not required to repackage an item unless the contents are fragile and would be at risk of damage during processing and transit.

Below are a few typical questions and answers:

Q. Is tape allowed?

A. Yes, tape is allowed on the seams and flaps of an FRE or FRB. Tape is allowed to reinforce the flaps of an FRE within its normal folds and of course to properly close a FRB.

---

[3] From the United States Postal Service (USPS) website
https://about.usps.com/postal-bulletin/2016/pb22435/html/updt_002.htm

Q. How much tape is acceptable?

A. Tape is permissible as reinforcement on the seams and flaps of a FRE or FRB to make sure the container does not break open during processing and transit. However, tape should not "encase" the FRE or FRB. Note that if a customer is using a printed Click-N-Ship® label or PC Postage Vendor label, extra tape is allowed to properly attach it to the envelope or box.

Q. What about bulges?

A. As long as the FRE or FRB can close "within the normal folds," bulges are not a problem. "Flat" refers to the price, not to the shape.

Q. What if the FRE is too thick?

A. There is currently no maximum thickness for a FRE. "Flat" refers to the price, not to the shape.

Q. What if the FRE is stuffed so full that it's shaped like a cylinder?

A. As long as the FRE can close within its normal folds, and as long as the sides of the FRE haven't been reconstructed, for example by being slit and having a gusset inserted, it is fine. "Flat" refers to the price, not to the shape.

Q. What if a skillet is packed in an FRB and the handle sticks out?

A. A small bump-out of the box is okay, but if the handle actually sticks out of the box or the box is reconfigured to accommodate the skillet, it cannot be considered as a FRB.

— Product Classification,
Pricing, 2-18-16

Addendum 3

Sourcing BOLOs

BOLO is an acronym for Be On the Look Out. They're lists of items to look for as you source at thrift stores, yard sales or the clearance aisle at your favorite box store. Your mileage may vary but many sellers have been pleased with their return on some of the items.

Always check recent sales before making a purchase. In general, avoid popular brands like Tommy Hilfiger, Chaps and Nautica. They sell but you may have 100s of competing sellers offering the same thing.

Books

    Chilton repair manuals
    First Editions (classics)
    Genealogy and Family/Regional Histories (the older, the better)
    Textbooks (current only)
    Yearbooks (varies with school and whether there were celebrities)

        In general, non-fiction does better than fiction or children's books

Electronics

> Amazon (especially the current version Echo Dots, FireTV and FireTV Cubes)
> Apple (check first to be sure you can sell online!)
> Bose
> Google (especially Glass and Home Hub)
> Go Pro
> Netgear
> Nintendo (especially classic)
> Ring Door Bell Video Cameras (later versions)
> Vintage equipment (e.g., cameras, handheld games, boom boxes, VHS players, rewinders, etc.)

Men's Clothing

> 5.11 Tactical
> Adidas (varies)
> Armani
> BAPE "A Bathing Ape" graphic t-shirts
> Brooks Brothers
> Burberry
> Carhart jackets
> Columbia PFG shirts
> Fire retardant clothing
> Harley Davidson (varies)
> Huk fishing shorts
> Nike (clothing and shoes … varies)
> Tiger Woods (Nike Golf)
> Tommy Bahama tropical shirts
> Trump ties and clothing
> Under Armor
> Western shirts

Toys

    Disney (varies)
    Erector
    K'nex
    Legos
    Lincoln Logs
    Magic the Gathering trading cards (varies)
    Pokemon trading cards (varies)
    Star Wars (varies)

Women's Clothing

    Athletic wear (tennis, yoga, leggings, sports bras, etc. … varies)
    Boots (western and rain … genuine leather boots sell best)
    Coach
    Denim jeans (especially unique and vintage)
    Eileen Fisher
    Ivanka Trump
    Kate Spade
    Nike (clothing and shoes … varies)
    Prada Shoes
    Rag and Bone jeans
    Versace (varies)

Miscellaneous

Cartridges, toner and filters (varies and best if not expired)
Dyson vacuums
Equestrian
Kitchen Aid appliances
Lowrance fish finders
Oakley
Movie posters
Ninja appliances
Ray Ban
Singer Sewing Machines (vintage)
Wetsuits
Yeti

Addendum 4

Supplies and Equipment

Sooner or later, the following supplies and equipment will prove handy. The good news is many of the items are already available in many households.

Photography

- Camera (with adequate lighting, most current smartphones work great)
- Lightbox (32" cube is capable of containing most items)
- Lights

Prepping

- Adhesive removal spray (e.g., Goo Gone)
- Adhesive removal tool (e.g., Scotty Peeler)
- Fuzz (pilling) removal tool
- Gloves (disposable)
- Polish (leather, shoe, etc. based on your inventory)

Printing

- Multifunction Laser Printer (capable of printing quality labels and scanning ... an alternative is a dedicated scanner and label printer)

Shipping Supplies

- Air pillows
- Bubble wrap
- Cardboard boxes (sized to ship your typical inventory)
- Shipping Labels
- Tape
- Tape Dispenser
- USPS Priority mailers and boxes (free from USPS)
- White poly (unlined) mailers
- White poly padded mailers

Software

- Financial tracking (spreadsheet, QuickBooks, Wave, etc.)
- Photo editing (free Google Picasso works for most situations)
- Presentation (e.g., Microsoft PowerPoint, Google Slides or Open Office)
- Spreadsheet (e.g., Microsoft Excel, Google Sheets or Open Office)

Sourcing

- Smartphone (capable of scanning bar codes to be researched on eBay)

About the Authors

Mike and Kay Chambers are an eBay Top Rated
Seller husband and wife team. Mike grew up in the
business world with Fortune 500 companies. He
has had leadership responsibilities at both the
facility and corporate levels. Mary Katherine
"Kay" Chambers is a career educator and small
business owner. At one time, Kay owned a brick-
and-mortar bookstore. Together, they have been
selling online for well over a decade.

Kay earned a bachelor's degree in secondary education from Ouachita Baptist
University and two master's degrees in education from the University of
South Carolina.

Mike graduated in electrical engineering from Auburn University. He has
done graduate work at both Auburn and Louisiana State Universities. He is
also a licensed electrician and professionally certified in maintenance,
reliability and continuous improvement.

In coaching others, Kay and Mike use their results-oriented experience and
hands-on backgrounds to help define a common sense, people-friendly
philosophy of leading and implementing change. Their goal is to not only
help provide the tools and insight to improve your eBay business but to also

generate quick results and help create a long-term learning approach that will help online and in life.

Kay has served with numerous civic and community organizations including the American Red Cross, Big Brothers Big Sisters of America, the Abused Women and Children of Clark County, the American Cancer Society and the Arkansas Baptist Children's Home. She has also participated in several inner-city mission programs around the United States helping impoverished children in Washington, D.C.; Houston, TX; Little Rock, AR; Tulsa, OK; and Atlanta, GA. Mike is a present or past member of the American Society for Quality (Senior Member, Section Chair, and Education Chair), County United Way Board of Directors (President), Rotary International, State Arthritis Board of Directors, County Rape and Violence Board of Directors, and Homeowners Association Board of Directors (Vice President).

Index

_F_

www.ingramcontent.com/pod-product-compliance
Lightning Source LLC
Chambersburg PA
CBHW052326220526

45472CB00001B/285